PAPER PEOPLE

PAPER PEOPLE

Michael Grater

"Stunning and highly imaginative," said *Scholastic Teacher* of Michael Grater's previous book on masks, PAPER FACES. Presently a teacher of craft techniques at a London college, the author's latest and equally imaginative offering, PAPER PEOPLE, explores some of the highly creative ways in which human figures of all kinds—clowns, witches, kings, queens, courtiers, knights, acrobats, strong men, angels, athletes, to name but a few—can easily be cut, folded or molded by using inexpensive sheets of construction or wrapping paper, aluminum foil or newspaper. Finishing touches may be added with crayons, paints, and odd scraps of brightly colored materials. The result is a delightful, challenging and endlessly amusing gallery of novel hand, finger, and glove puppets, marionettes, mobiles, jumping jacks, standing figures, ornaments and irresistible action toys. Each project offers extensive opportunity for improvisation by the older child or by a parent, teacher, or youth leader to meet a given situation, for each idea or technique opens the way to a dozen others.

Illustrated throughout with helpful photographs of Michael Grater's own PAPER PEOPLE and with many clear, step-by-step drawings, this fanciful volume promises to become one of the most useful and popular paper-craft books ever published.

PAPER PEOPLE

by MICHAEL GRATER

illustrated by the author

photographs by Geoffrey Goode

TAPLINGER PUBLISHING COMPANY
New York

First Published in the United States in 1970 by
TAPLINGER PUBLISHING CO., INC.
29 East Tenth Street
New York, New York 10003

SBN 8008-6255-4

Library of Congress Catalog Card Number 77-99308

Printed in the United States of America

CONTENTS

Paper People

Paper People is, as you would expect, about paper and about people. It explores some of the creative opportunities which might occur when the two are put together.

Paper and cardboard are materials which are easily available today—in an ever-widening range of quality and style—and which can be used creatively with a minimum of equipment or special facilities.

If you attempt any of the work suggested, or if you want to use it as a point of departure for trying out ideas of your own, you have only to find the material and to provide yourself with some means of cutting and fixing it.

Papers and cardboard can be bought in a variety of colours and patterns, or they can often be salvaged from the mass of packaging which comes into our homes every day. It is impossible to list the types of both which might be used for the work. In most cases they will need to be adequately strong. But this will never be stronger than a whole range of papers and cardboard which are generally available.

Where decorative effects are suggested any of the attractive gift wrapping papers which are available can be used in combination with plainer types such as cartridge or brushwork paper.

Cardboard, which may be expensive to buy, can be salvaged from cartons and protective wrappings.

For cutting the materials, scissors will normally be adequate, although occasionally the reader might prefer to use a knife for a particular process. There

are many different sorts of knife available today for modelling and hobbies, and the best sort to use will be the type supplied with throw-away blades. These can be bought quite cheaply, as can the replacement blades. If a knife is used a special cutting surface may be necessary. This can be a board with a piece of cheaper cardboard pinned to its surface. The cardboard can be renewed from time to time.

For fixing the materials various adhesives are available which are suitable for papers and cardboard. The best of these are instant glues which are normally applied to both surfaces and allowed to dry slightly before they are put together.

A small office hand stapler is an invaluable addition to the working equipment. Its use can make fixtures simple, as well as immediate and permanent.

Paints of various sorts, oil crayons, or felt pens will be found useful throughout the work.

The work suggested is generally light-hearted and not very serious. Working in paper is a simple and unpretentious craft. It is a fun activity, which can be amusing and mildly idiotic, but which can at the same time be creatively rewarding because there are so many things which can be made in the material.

If we paused to consider the things we do we might often find ourselves remembering the things we have made. We find it easy to remember making them, and we remember the further experiences of using them and having them around us, because the things we make usually give us pleasure.

In this time when we have so many ready-made things thrust at us, it might be meaningful to look for as many opportunities as we can to make things for ourselves. There are a number of simple items included in the following pages which might be called toys and which—in an age of plastics and precision models —might seem quaint and old-fashioned.

These have been deliberately included because when everything is manufactured with such a high degree of skill and excellence we might forget some things which in their own way were also good.

If we do not make things for ourselves we might never know some of the simple pleasures which children used to know—and this could be a real loss!

Newspaper Figures

To make things we must start with materials, and we must find the special tools and skills which will help us to manipulate these materials.

If we start with paper, and if we think about people and the human figure, we will probably find ourselves, through habit, looking for a pencil or for something to draw with. We are used to making a line on paper, and we are further used to making this line into a shape which tells us something. Drawing and paper are two things which go together. They make a happy combination and can give us a great deal of pleasure.

But there are problems.

Draw someone you know—or any human figure!

If we were very young and were asked to do this, we would probably attempt it without a second thought. A small circle on a larger circle would do for the head and body, stick strokes for legs and arms, with dots for eyes and simple marks for the nose and mouth. It would be enough—if we were very young.

As we grow older we like to improve our drawings. We like them to be 'good' drawings, which usually means that we like them to be accurate and detailed. If we want our drawings to improve in this way we must, as we grow more aware of the things we want to portray, develop a suitably skilled technique. We think we know what a good drawing should be like, and what is needed from the artist.

But some of us do not quite succeed. We are quickly aware that our drawings seem to be inadequate or wrong. When we try to draw a figure it remains stiff and lifeless. The head is too small and does not quite fit the body, or the arms are too long. The line we are using somehow refuses to behave as we want it to.

To make matters worse for us we see other people's drawings, and we are often aware that they are better than ours. We are no longer satisfied with the drawings we used to do with such pleasure when we were very young. We want to make our drawings better and more like the real thing, because we come to believe that this is what they should be like.

But if we cannot develop the appropriate skill, and if we are unable to reach this standard, drawing ceases to be fun.

This is a pity, since there are no rules anywhere which either tell us what drawing is, or which define the standard it ought to reach at any given age.

If we appear not to be successful in one method we can sometimes get satisfaction by working in another way.

We might try drawing in a different way.

You can try this as a first exercise.

You can start with a sheet of newspaper—a single sheet, not a whole double page.

If you fold it through the middle and tear it into two pieces, this will give you a convenient size to start with.

Fold one of the pieces longways into two again, and without drawing, try to tear the outside edge in the shape of a figure. You must think as you tear, and you must look hard at the paper.

When you have finished tearing you can open the paper out flat (Fig. 1).

The first time you do this might well be a disaster, but you can practise it because it will cost you nothing.

When you do it again, after folding, start at the top of the head and work down the outside shape, tearing a little at a time between the forefinger and thumb of both hands. In this way you will find that you have more control over the way the tear goes.

The second time should be an improvement on the first. But you must look at the result and you must think. Is it obviously a human figure? You are not concerned with whether or not it is good. Is it just a torn piece of newspaper? Or does it say something about the human figure? You can only tell by looking.

Are the proportions disastrous, or are they somewhere near right? Are the arms, for example, long enough? Where do they reach at the side of the body? If you are not sure, you can stand up and compare them with your own. What do your fingers touch when your arms are at your sides?

If you stand up and try this it will tell you something. And it will tell you something which you need to know. It will tell you about human proportion, and you can relate this to the figure you have 'drawn' in newspaper. Are the proportions of your torn figure fairly accurate? Or do you need to try again?

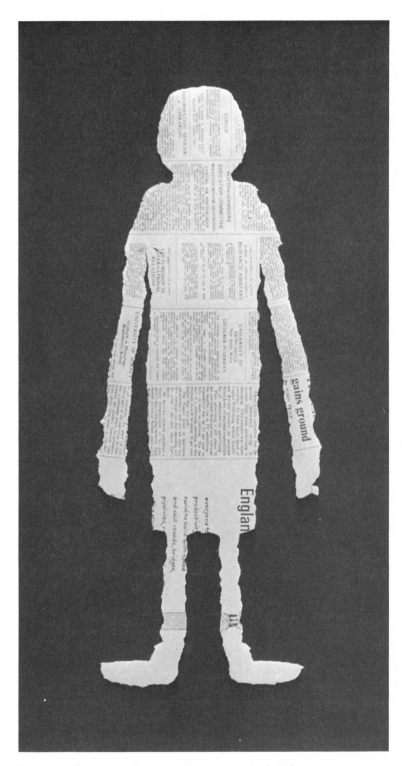

Fig. 1 The first paper figure can be torn on the fold from newspaper.

Fig. 2 With practice you should be able to tear a number of figures together.

You can tear more of these figures until you are able to make a shape which might be reasonably acceptable as a human figure. If you practise a little you will learn something. You will first of all learn something about the material. Then you will learn something about controlling it and making it do what you want it to.

Although there is no rule which says you must not do so, it is best at this stage not to try drawing the figure before you tear. Drawing is a special technique, and although it has a very real place in many of the things we do, it may not be the only way of finding or recording a shape. In this exercise, instead of the pencil point, you are using the tips of your fingers. And you should be looking hard at the shapes you make.

When you think you are able to tear an adequate shape for a human figure, you can experiment with folding your paper so that you can produce a number of figures at the same time. These are separate figures. They are not joined together, and the number you can produce effectively will depend on the strength of your fingers. If you tear the paper the slightest bit at a time it should be possible to make three or four figures in one go (Fig. 2).

When you have a number of these you can do another type of drawing with them. You can place them on a flat surface, and can manipulate them into various positions.

If you look at the two figures illustrated (Fig. 3), you will see that although they were the ones torn in the previous example, they have now been manipulated or arranged to communicate a particular movement.

You can try this with some of your own figures. Can you make a figure run? Or can you make it sit down? Can you make the figure stand on its head? You can fold or tear or rearrange the figure in any way you like.

You can put figures together. You can put two of them together so that they appear to be fighting. You can make one sag at the knees, as though he has just received a particularly hard blow.

If you have a large piece of paper in front of you, you can place a lot of figures in various positions all over it. You can have the figures still or moving— running or jumping. You can have them standing,

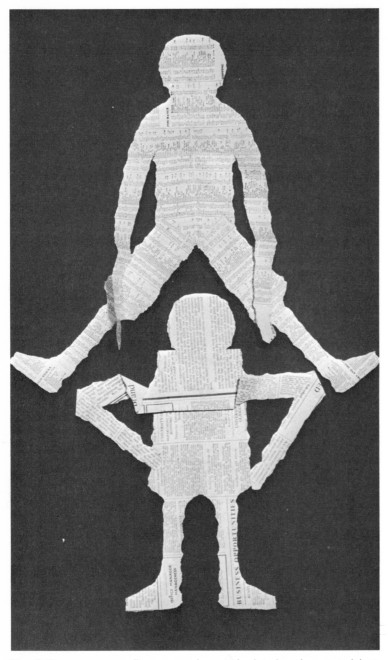

Fig. 3 The newspaper figures can be manipulated and arranged in a number of ways.

kneeling or lying down.

When you have found some interesting combinations of figures, you might take some paste—water-mixed paste will be best—and stick the figures flat on the background. When you stick them down you must keep them in the positions you have decided on. Although you might fold or tear them in order to put them in position you should paste them down as flat as possible.

After sticking the figures you can paint them as you would paint an ordinary picture. You can paint their features and clothes, and the background. If your pigment is fairly thick, and you managed to paste the figures flat, it will not be too apparent in the final version of the picture that you have used a method any different from normal.

Is this drawing? It does not really matter. What you have done is to find a way of making shapes which represent something. In this case you have used them on a background. It might not be drawing, although you actually made a line when you were tearing the folded paper. But whatever it is, you should have ended up with what you set out to make—a number of people in paper. You are developing a skill, and you can prove this by subjecting yourself to a more difficult situation.

Newspaper Figure Pictures

You might take a very complex situation with lots of human figures in all sorts of action poses. You can take as a subject—a violent battle scene. This is not easy to draw. But you should now have the beginnings of a skill which will really make it possible for you to tackle the subject in business-like way.

To do this you will need lots of newspapers and the largest piece of background paper you can find.

For a background you might stick together a number of sheets of wrapping paper. If you can collect some of these, you can stick them together with the type of brown gummed strip which you can buy in the roll.

If you are working in your own room you could make this background the same size as the door, which you could then use as an easel or working surface. Try to make it as large as the door. It can stay up there for a few days while you work on it, and it is not likely to be in anyone's way.

Now mix a large jar of paste, and tear lots of newspaper figures. When you tear them you can vary the sizes from the largest possible in the newspaper sheet, to the smallest you can manage with your fingers.

If you make a thick pad of newspaper as a surface to paste on you will avoid unnecessary mess. When you have done this you can start straight away pasting and sticking the figures.

As you paste them on the background make them fight. Choose a period of history in which there was a battle, and imagine the confusion and general chaos.

The paste, as you have seen, will make the figures malleable so that you can make them run or leap or stagger or fall—or do anything which figures might do in a battle.

Sometimes you can stick figures partly over others. You would never see them all separate with a space between them.

As you stick the figures you can smooth them down with the brush or with your fingers. You can tear them and rearrange them. You can put some together in tight groups, and others can be struggling together in pairs.

It will take you an hour or two to do this, but as you work and the scene develops, you might pause occasionally to step back and see it from a distance.

The effect should be dramatic—even if you cannot draw very well in the normal way. It might be even more dramatic if you start on a pre-coloured background. A few sheets of newspaper stuck together, or wrapping paper, can be immediately and effectively coloured with sheets of tissue paper, which can be pasted on before the figures.

For a battle scene a red tissue sky will add a startling note to the over-all effect, and will create the right atmosphere for the scene you are depicting with your figures.

You might notice, as you place the figures, that the use of different-sized ones will begin to introduce a scale into the picture. The larger figures will be nearer, and the smaller ones away in the distance. You might be able to use this factor to advantage if you are interested, in which case you will want to group larger figures to the foreground with others going away smaller into the distance.

When you have pasted all your figures in position you can add colour in any areas you like. The picture will be ready for painting. But if you do paint it, work all over it. This is likely to be more effective than working slowly outwards from one position.

Other subjects can be just as suitable for this treatment. You might not be interested in battle scenes, so you must consider alternative subjects.

The technique is obviously suitable for subjects in which there are lots of people, so that any crowd scene can be attempted:

Children playing in the park.

A football match or any other sporting event—a cross-country run is a good subject if you have a long thin panel to work on.

A procession or any scene from history which would have collected a crowd.

You could make a family group of your own family at a special occasion—a wedding, for example. It might be interesting to include every member of the family and to watch their reactions as they sort themselves out from the finished work.

There are many stories and poems which you might illustrate with this technique.

The Pied Piper of Hamelin would be very suitable, done on a long piece of frieze or ceiling paper.

There are many Bible stories which would make exciting subjects.

There are, in fact, so many stories from all sorts of different sources which concern masses of people. And so many situations which you must have experienced personally in which crowds gather together for some purpose. The range of subjects is so extensive that listing them would take up far too much space. And in any case it is better for you to think about the technique, and then to make your own decision.

After the picture treatment of some of these newspaper figures it might be possible to experiment with a fun or simple patterned effect. If you were not inter-

12 ested in making a picture you could still tear some of the figures, and could use them for a decoration. You could try:

Striped figures.

Figures with coloured circles all over—like bubbles. These could be painted on or stuck with coloured paper, or they could be printed on, using corks or some other suitable block.

Figures with blots of ink in various colours spreading from the central fold.

Figures pasted all over with a collage of postage stamps, or with colourful sweet wrappings.

Any of these, and others which you might discover for yourself, could be pinned around the walls as a decoration, or even pinned to the ceiling so that they hang freely. Although in this case your figures would have to be decorated on both sides, because you would in fact have made them three-dimensional—or very simple examples of sculpture in paper.

It is possible to develop the torn paper figures which you have just been playing with into simple sculpture.

They will never, of course, be great sculpture, but they can be an interesting introduction to the way in which your material can be made to take on new forms.

If you stretch a piece of string at a reasonable level across your room, making sure that it is out of the way of anyone who might walk in without looking, you can hang some of the newspaper figures from it.

To start with you can try making a figure hang by two hands. It should look as though the figure is hauling himself hand-over-hand across a wide gap.

You can now make him hang precariously from one hand.

If you can do this, it is a very simple form of sculpture. Like the drawing you did previously with the figures it is not the same as the real thing, but it is legitimate enough—especially if you are learning as you work.

You can make your attempts at sculpture more purposeful if you like. You can hang one figure upside down, folding his knees over the string. You can now make him hold a second hanging figure by the hands,

Sculptured Newspaper Figures

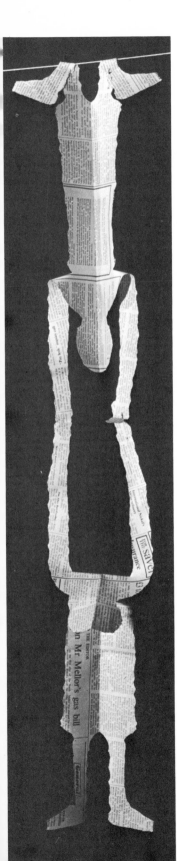

Fig. 4 Simple experiments in form can be made with the newspaper figures.

13

which might in a very simple way communicate the idea of trapeze artists (Fig. 4).

This simple piece of modelling is developed more fully in a later exercise, but if you want to, you can take it on from this point for yourself.

Can you make the top figure, for example, hold the lower one from the ankles? In both cases your manipulation of the torn newspaper figures will result in a simple type of sculpture. You should look at the material as you work with it, noticing the way it bends and takes a form, or the way the fold seems to keep the body stiff.

The torn newspaper figures can be developed also by sticking them to stiff cardboard and then, after cutting the outer shape, mounting the cards on wooden blocks so that the figures will stand freely.

The players in the illustration (Fig. 5) were torn originally from newspaper, like the one on the extreme left, and were then pasted to cardboard. They were then stapled at the foot to cuts of scrapwood. In some cases a further piece of wood was stapled up the back of the figure from the base, to give extra support where it was needed.

You could make your own favourite team in this way, giving each figure the individual character of one of the players. You might even develop a game with a friend who could make an opposing team. You would have to make up your own rules, but you could discuss these and decide on them between yourselves.

If you made your own favourite team you might place them around your room, altering their positions according to their respective performances at the matches they played. If you are really interested in something you will be pleased to be involved in it as fully as possible.

If you do not happen to have a favourite team you might make a version of the school team in this way. You could make and award them rosettes for the goals they score. You might even persuade your teacher to let you have this version of the team displayed some-

14

Fig. 5 The newspaper figures can be stuck to card and arranged to stand freely.

where in the school, and if you used the rosettes you would all be able to watch their respective progress throughout the season.

Although torn newspaper figures are about as simple as any figure could be they have a surprising potential. You have seen how they can be arranged in many ways to make pictures, or how they can be adapted as simple sculptures. One of their chief virtues is that the newsprint from which they are torn becomes malleable when it is pasted, and allows you to manipulate them into any sort of human position. In this respect the thinness of the paper is an advantage, but if a more durable figure is needed you must obviously use paper of a better quality.

There are so many different types and qualities of paper available today that it is not necessary to specify any one for any of the exercises suggested. After newsprint you have a range of parcel wrapping papers, all sorts of bought papers—both white and coloured—and various types of cardboard. Cartons and corrugated you can investigate when you need something stronger.

It is useful to get into the habit of saving papers and cardboard, and storing them for future use, even if you can think of nothing to use them for when first they become available. You will find it quite unnecessary to buy materials for most of the work suggested. If you search around, and ask in the right places, you should get most of your materials for no cost at all.

Cut Single Figures   If you have made some of the newspaper figures, and if you have managed to come by some stronger papers, you may still find pleasure in working with torn or cut-out shapes. These will still, of course, be mass shapes and not just figures drawn on a page.

With stronger paper it might be necessary to cut rather than tear the figures. But your work with the torn newspaper should have given you a feeling for shape, which is in this case the beginning of a skill with the material, and you should not find the difference impossibly difficult.

If you are going to cut, there is still no rule about drawing the figure first, although you ought not to find this necessary. If you want an outline to work from you can make a simple one, but you should fold the paper first through the middle so that you will only need to draw a half outline. And this will be very much related to the size of the paper you are going to cut.

If you are going to cut, it is a good idea to try to cut as little away as possible from your original paper, so that your figures will be as large and as simple as you can make them.

If you could develop the trapeze family which was suggested earlier, it might make an interesting painting exercise, and would also give you an opportunity to develop it as a sculptural group.

In this case, since the figures would be stronger, you might make simple trapezes for them, using drinking straws and cotton. You might also put them together in more varied ways (Fig. 6). They can be seated or they can hang, or they might even be strong enough to stand holding the cotton supports.

16

Fig. 6 The cut figures, given identity, can be decorated and assembled in various ways.

Fig. 7 Added features may be cut from different papers and combined with the original shape.

You can paint or crayon the features and costumes of the figures, giving each one an identity. You can also string the whole group together, and hang them somewhere so that they will move gently all the time. In order to make any movement effective you should aim, when stringing the group together, to have one final string at the top. This would mean that two groups would have to have a piece of thin wood between them, with one string from the point of balance.

Other figures can be attempted in the same way— that is by folding the paper through the centre and cutting away as little as possible.

Simple witch shapes could make an attractive decoration for Halloween. These would be very suitable for a bold patterned treatment, and it would not be unreasonable to find them suspended in mid-air.

The witches illustrated (Fig. 7) are a little different from earlier shapes. They have painted or added paper decorations, and they have additional cut pieces for hair. The broomstick with paper brush can be pierced through the body, and the arms can be stapled to the broom handle which can be made from a thin piece of dowel or garden cane.

To make a decoration like this it is useful to begin with variations in the paper you start with. This can be of different colours, and the pieces from which the witches are to be cut can be of different proportions and sizes. In this way you will get fat witches and thin witches, as well as light and dark ones, which might add interest to the decoration.

Many of the suggestions which follow might also be suitable for use as decorations, so at this point you might consider some of the simple ways of making sure that a decoration will be effective. There are no rules, of course, and decorations of any sort will be bound to have your own personal touch, but in general some things are desirable.

They should be attractive in colour. Drab or dirty colours are unfortunately only too easy to mix. But if they do occur when you are working you must reject them immediately.

A colour control is also useful in the over-all effect of a decoration. If you hang a number of units, like the witches for example, you could make them from as many different colours as you could find papers. But if before you started you decided not to have too many different colours, you could make a deliberate choice for the decoration. You could have them perhaps all in different tones of red, so that the impact would be immediate when anyone walked into the room. Or you could have them in black and white with red. There are as many different possibilities as there are colours. It is the way you select them and put them together which is important.

The actual shape of the units you use in a decoration

is also important. This is usually best when it is simple and uncluttered. Snipping cuts with the scissors, which make small edge patterns, may appear right when you are working with the shape close to you, but the effect might be meaningless when the shape is seen from a distance.

If you are going to cut the edge of any shape, or if you are going to cut any part of it, you should try to control your cutting so that the effect is as simple and immediate as possible.

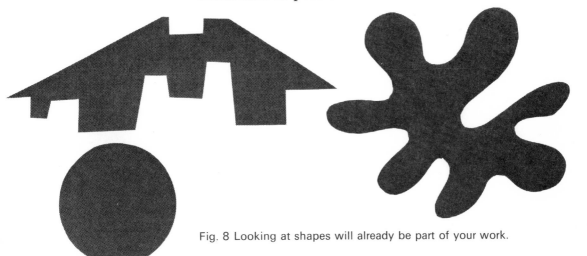

Fig. 8 Looking at shapes will already be part of your work.

Of the three shapes (Fig. 8) one is clearly much simpler than the other two. You can try looking at the example for a moment and then closing your eyes. Which shape can you most clearly remember or recreate? And what about the others? You should not look back at the illustration, but you should think about the shapes. Were all the edges of either one curved or square? How many projections were there at the edges? You are not likely to remember such details. It would take a real effort of looking and thinking even to begin to make the shapes memorable.

A decoration should demand no effort. It should be a background thing of immediate appeal. Decorations are after all only intended to be backgrounds to something else—to a party or special occasion. They are there to brighten the scene, not to make it clever and complicated.

The way you decorate the witches or any other figures you might make is a matter for personal choice.

You can begin by deciding on a style of decoration and you can carry it out in the idiom you have chosen. Or you can start, hoping that something good will emerge as you work.

There are many different styles of decoration and pattern treatment. You will see this if you look around you, deliberately comparing the way things have been decorated, and it is unlikely that you will need to worry much about finding styles of your own. They will soon come to you.

The same will apply to the shapes you make. At first, before you have real confidence, you might copy some of the shapes illustrated. But this should occur less and less as you become aware of the nature of the materials you use. The illustrations are there to help you understand the text, because obviously when you are reading about shapes it could be difficult to visualize them from words alone.

In some cases diagrams are actually included with an outline. But these again are only intended to make the process of construction clearer. If you can improve or make any of your own variations on the examples shown, you should do so. The intention is to support your work as you learn and as you develop skill with the material.

It is, however, desirable that as you develop a feeling for the material you will at the same time be developing a decorative ability. As the shapes change through your handling of the material, you will need to extend your fluency with patterns and colours. You must think as you work. What can you do with patterns? How can you, for example, use a striped pattern? You might cut a simple paper figure, preferably as large as possible, and you might see how many different stripes you can put on it.

You could have thin or thick stripes, or a mixture of both. They could be vertical, horizontal or diagonal. They could be straight or curved. They could be thin at one point and thicker at another, (Fig. 9). And what you can do with stripes you can do with other sorts of pattern.

Fig. 9 There are many different ways of putting stripes on a figure.

As you work you will discover new and exciting things about colours and shapes. You will not remember all of them at the same time, so that if asked to do so you could recite everything you know. This is not the intention.

When you are working you will want to make your work as attractive as possible. And to do this you need a storehouse from which you can draw ideas, which will then be fed back into the storehouse as you work. It is a process which goes on all the time. But it is one you must really undertake for yourself.

Many things happen when we put colours together. If we were to write down all the different colour-mixing possibilities, the list would be as long as this page. But you would not learn much from the list alone. You must work with colour if you want to know about it; and the same with shape. But as you work it can be fun, and the things you do can give pleasure to others.

When you have torn some figures and cut others you will have experienced two different qualities in the way the material can be used. The torn figures will tend to be softer in general effect than the cut ones. If you can see this you are already beginning to appreciate something about the nature of the material, and this is essential in the development of ability in any craft. To develop your awareness more fully you might try tearing and cutting figures from all sorts of paper.

When you unwrap something—it can be as small as an orange or it can be a very large parcel—try folding the paper and tearing a figure. This can be an amusing pastime. You can do it in restaurants after your parents have paid the bill. You can do it when you are visiting friends, or on any occasion when you are handed a piece of paper—if the paper is unimportant. It can be fun, and it will all be part of your developing skill.

Full-size Paper Figures

If you can find a very large sheet of paper—it might be wrapping paper or paper from a continuous roll, like wallpaper—you can try tearing or cutting your own shape full-size. You can fold it through the middle, using the floor as a working surface, and you can tear the shape at the edge, inch by inch. You will probably be surprised when you open it out and see what you think you look like.

For an interesting comparison you can get a second large sheet and find a friend who will draw round you while you lie on it. After the friend has made the drawing you can tear it out and put the two shapes side by side. You can then paint the shapes and pin them to a wall. If you only use a fixture at the top, your shapes might curl slightly and take a little form. In which case they will make shadows behind the shapes which might add to the general effect.

Full-size paper figures can make a very strong decoration. This means that you will only need a few of them, whereas with a smaller unit you might need more to make an adequate background. The very size of these figures, especially if they were decorated in gay colours, would make a striking effect. You could pin them to doors, or you could bend them and make them sit in corners or at the top of the stairs.

If you have paints or colouring materials which are not really large enough for you to cope with work this size, you might make a coloured effect with tissue paper. This is available in a great variety of colours, and can be torn and pasted to a background to make an immediate colour impact. If you can get a range of tissue papers you might tear strips for the large figures and stick them on overlapping, so that you will get different tones where there is more than one thickness.

There are many different colour treatments you can make with tissue paper. You can cut or tear it in different shapes. These can be regular or irregular, squares, circles, triangles and others which you can find for yourself. You can spiral the paper, because it is soft like newspaper and can be modelled when it is pasted. You can arrange it in zigzags, curves or sharp angles. You can make patterns which grow from the centre like stars or the sun, or you can make the pattern grow in other directions.

If you make one full-size figure this year, and you put this away until you make another next year, it might be interesting to see how much you have grown yourself. Full-size figures are simple to make, and are

Dancing Dollies Most of you will at some time have folded papers and cut out the lines of figures which are called Dancing Dollies. If you have never done this, or have done it and forgotten how, you might go on from the single figures into various arrangements of figures together.

There are a number of different ways in which the paper can be folded and cut. If you work through them with a systematic approach you will soon know the basic ones, and can go on from this point as you like.

You should begin with a rectangle of fairly thin paper, placed on the working surface in front of you with the longer side as the horizontal.

You should now:

Fold it in half through the centre—like a book.

Fold it in half again.

And fold it in half again—so that you have made the original into eight pieces, (Fig. 10).

You can now draw half a figure, but you must place it so that *the arm is at the original centre fold*, (Fig. 10).

When you cut this line and open out the paper you will have a row of Dancing Dollies (Fig. 11). If you have not started by making the end of the arm touch the centre fold, you will probably end up with half figures at the ends when you open the paper.

This row of Dancing Dollies can of course be different in many ways from the one illustrated. You can experiment when you draw the shapes, comparing the effectiveness of the results when you open the folds.

If you can find a paper thin enough but still adequately strong, you can try introducing more folds so that you will end up with more figures.

When you have tried the figures as a straight line, you can experiment by folding the paper in different ways before cutting.

The diagram (Fig. 12) shows a square of paper:

Folded once on a diagonal—to make a triangle.

Folded again into a smaller triangle.

Folded double again—so that you again have eight pieces, in this case triangles.

C

24

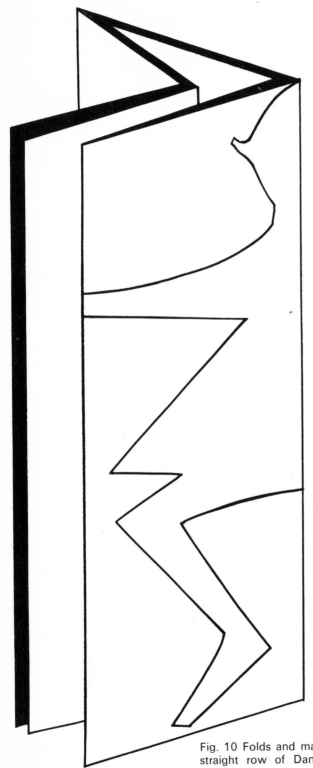

Fig. 10 Folds and marking for the
straight row of Dancing Dollies.

Fig. 11 The number of Dollies will depend on how many folds you make.

Two alternative methods of cutting are illustrated in the diagram.

The continuous line making half a figure—you can follow this with the point of a pencil if you are in any doubt—has the head to the folded point of all the triangles. If you look at the diagram carefully you will be able to see from the toned areas how the paper is folded.

If you draw and cut the figure illustrated with an unbroken line you will find, on opening the paper, that your dollies are dancing in a circle (Fig. 13).

If you try this a second time, this time drawing a full figure—like the one illustrated with a dotted line, which has the head to the outside edge of the folds—you should find eight dollies when you open the paper. These might have an interesting pattern at the legs (Fig. 14). These dollies can be cut from plain paper as in the illustration, but cut from patterned paper they can make most attractive place-mats for a party or for a special family meal.

Fig. 12 When the Dollies are cut from a folded square various placings of the figure are possible.

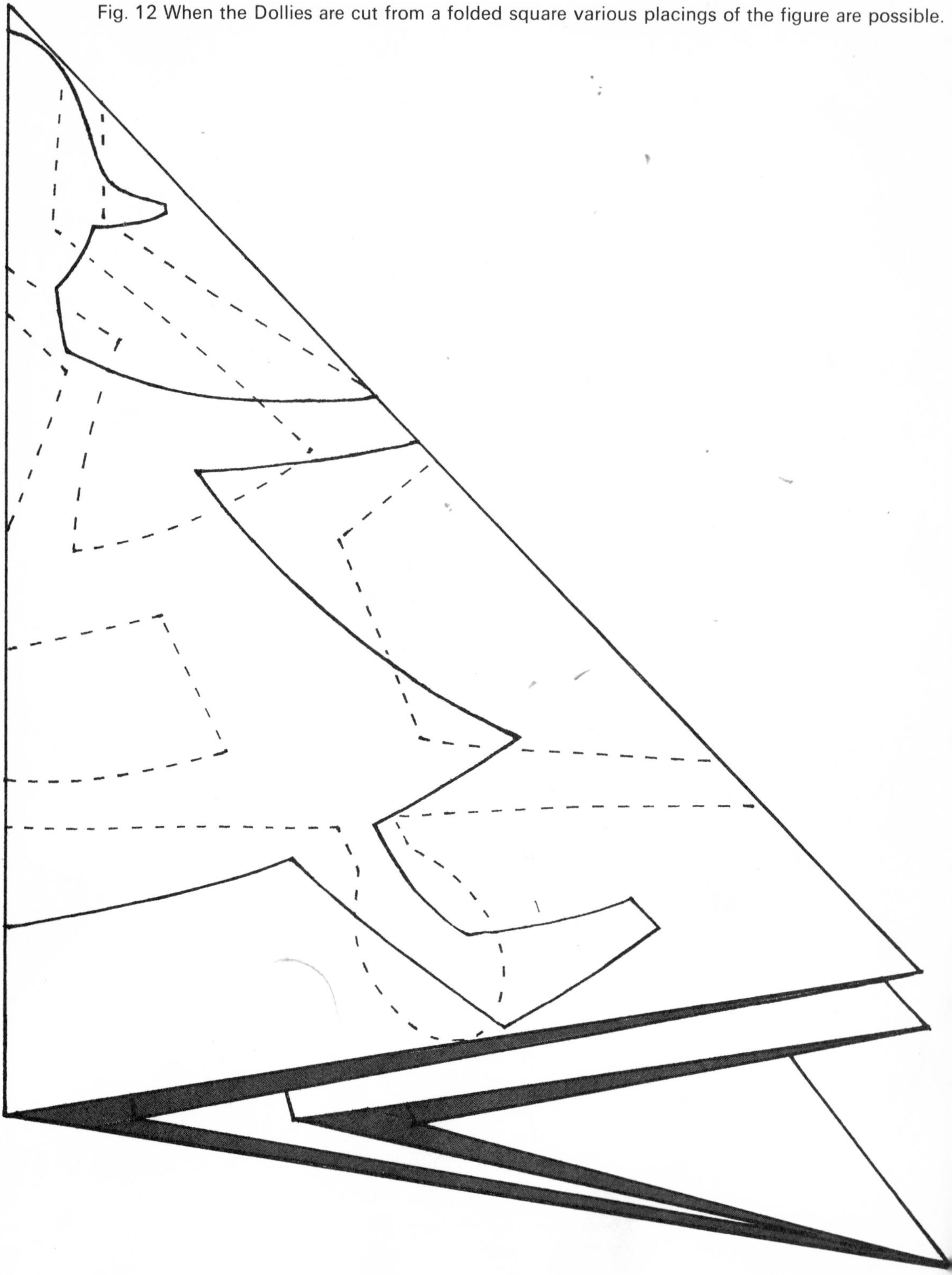

Fig. 13 A half shape on the square will result in four figures.

Fig. 14 A whole shape on the square will result in eight figures.

Patterned papers can be found now in a marvellous variety of styles. You will have received birthday and Christmas presents wrapped in these special papers, and you will appreciate by now why they should never be ripped off—even if you are in a hurry to get to the present. You will find all sorts of uses for these papers as you work in many of the exercises, and you should try to get into the habit of unwrapping your parcels carefully and preserving the papers.

Dancing Dollies, which you make in patterned papers, will add a gay personal touch to your parties, and making them will add to the fun which is always involved in preparing for the party.

Joined Figures The technique of cutting a number of Dancing Dollies together can be extended to other subjects in order to make interesting figure groups.

The diagram (Fig. 15) illustrates a method of folding a long strip of paper. This could be about half the width of this page and about twice as long, although the actual size is not critical. You can try the exercise in any rectangle of paper which is obviously longer than it is wide.

If you place the paper on the working surface in front of you, vertical so that the longer sides extend away from you, you can fold the paper double—downwards from the top.

You can now fold it downwards again into two, making at this point four thicknesses, with the open ends at the bottom.

You can now fold the whole thing in half like a book, and can draw in a half figure (Fig. 15).

The figure may of course be any shape you please, but the arms should be drawn upwards so that the lowest figure can appear to support the others which will emerge from the cutting and opening out the original strip (Fig. 16).

An exercise like this, in which you can cut four or even six figures at a time, might make a lively group project for your classroom. You could suggest it to your teacher, and a group of you might work together until you had enough figures to stretch from floor to ceiling.

30

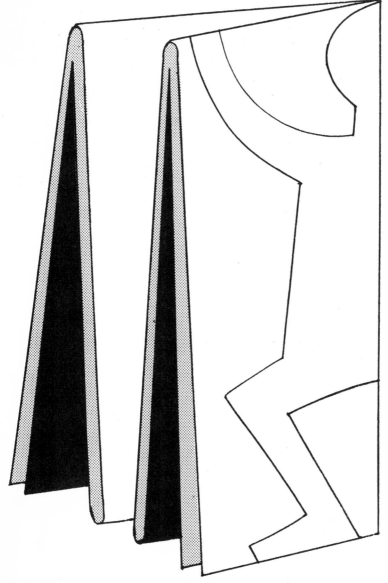

Fig. 15 The Dancing Dollies technique can be used in various ways.

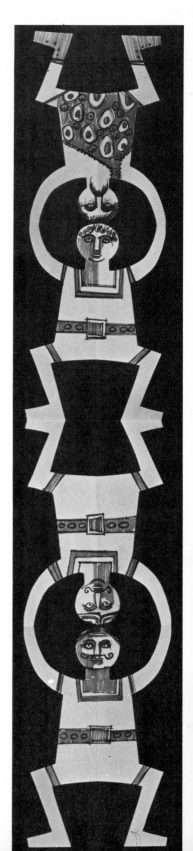

Fig. 16 A concertina fold, doubled, will result in a different placing of the figures.

Fig. 17 A simple repetition of figures is useful for fun exercises.

Fig. 18 They can be dressed in patterned aprons.

Patterns on the figures, and appropriate features, will add to the pleasure you will get from various developments with the Dancing Dollies technique.

A simple row of standing figures (Fig. 17) will provide lots of opportunity for decorating and dressing.

You could make them into likenesses of your neighbours, or of other people you know, and you could design and make for each one of them an overall or pinafore. It would be easy enough to cut out these shapes by folding coloured or decorated paper through the centre, and cutting the aprons with tabs at the top to fold over the original Joined Figures (Fig. 18).

As a class exercise you might interchange the aprons and hand them out like presents from one group to another. Or if you attempt something like this at home you could work with your friends. You might even design clothes and other accessories for the figures.

You could even use off-cuts of textile materials to dress the figures, although you would only need to cut and stick the material to the front of the figures. It would not be necessary to sew it.

There are various alternative ways in which you might amuse yourself and your friends with figures like this.

Besides dressing them you might set yourself up as a milliner, and might design and make extravagant hats (Fig. 19). For this you would need a basic shape to go on the top of the head, and a selection of bits and pieces—of felts and feathers and beads and sequins—which you could put together to make something you feel the character might choose.

If you are not interested in millinery you could have fun with your friends, or in your class, by making the figures hairless, and by making extravagant wigs (Fig. 20). These could have tabs for fixing over the tops of the heads, and could be in all sorts of different patterns and styles.

You might even cut a basic shape in paper or cardboard, and add something to this for hair. You could use wool or string, which—if you can find the right adhesive—you might be able to arrange in curls or in a style of your own invention.

Figures with interchangeable beards or moustaches might make an interesting project, or figures with

Fig. 19 Or gay hats!

Fig. 20 Or they can be made hairless with interchangeable wigs.

36 extravagant ties. You could make a row of supporters for your football club, and these could have the scarves and coloured accessories which team supporters like to wear.

If you dress the figures you can pin them flat to the wall, or you can use the centre fold so that they stand out a little away from the wall. This can be visually more interesting because of the shadows made between the folds.

Single-fold Standing Figures

In some of your work with the previous exercises you might have seen that a vertical fold through the centre of a piece of paper will give it added support and extra visual interest.

You can demonstrate this for yourself by taking any plain sheet of paper and trying to stand it on its edge. This is not possible. The paper will fall flat every time.

If you try this you might find yourself instinctively wanting to put a fold into the paper so that it will support itself. One vertical fold through the centre should be enough to make the sheet stand freely. The paper with the fold has become slightly stronger than it was when it was flat.

If you now stand the paper freely you will notice that it has two surfaces, or planes, which meet at the fold. Although these are actually the same colour they will now be different in tone. The plane nearer the source of light in the room will be lighter than the other.

It is this contrast in tone which can be used for effect when you are working with paper. It is doubly useful because, resulting from a fold, the paper is strengthened every time you use the technique.

After using this visual effect in some of your previous exercises you can introduce and use it deliberately with figures so that they will stand freely.

Single-fold Historical Figures

The study of history might at times seem to be a dull subject. But this should not be so. History is about people and the things they did—both the ordinary everyday things and more dramatic events. Since it is

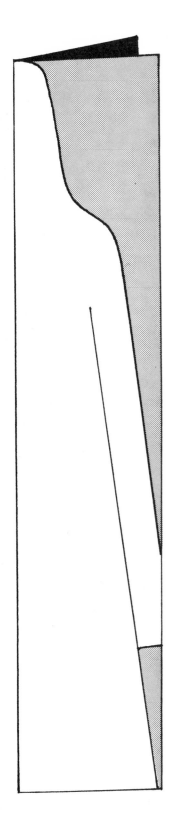

about people there must be many opportunities with paper or cardboard figures which might enliven a study of the subject.

Historical figures of almost any character or period can be developed on a simple figure cut from a single fold.

Since it might be required to support dressing and might have various equipments fixed to it, the figure is best made in cardboard. If you can buy it, an eight-sheet card would be about right; but various sorts of salvaged cardboard would do just as well.

The figure should be cut as a simple basic shape (Fig. 21). This will include arms which allow for slight manipulation, and it should be left as wide as possible at the base.

The simplest way of developing this figure is by drawing an identity on it and adding bits of equipment to give it more form.

The Norman soldiers (Fig. 22) are made of thin cardboard about twice the height of this page. The shape used is the basic one, with slight cut-away portions defining the legs. The wide base is still left, so that it gives the figures the largest possible point of support.

The main treatment is a simple drawn and painted version of what Norman soldiers might have looked like, with the details freely copied from a reference book. You can always find a suitable reference source at your school or local library. These are usually well illustrated, but it is not necessary for you to copy exactly or to attempt to imitate the illustration.

The way you draw or paint on your figure must be entirely a matter of how you are able to do it, not how someone else has done it. You must use the illustration as a reference to tell you what sort of garments or armour the particular figures you are concerned with might have worn.

It will help perhaps in this sort of figure construction if you use a felt-tipped pen to make a bold statement of the main characteristics before painting. This will include things like belts and bands of decoration, but the type of treatment you give your figures is entirely a matter of choice.

Fig. 21 For Standing Figures a wide base must be retained.

38

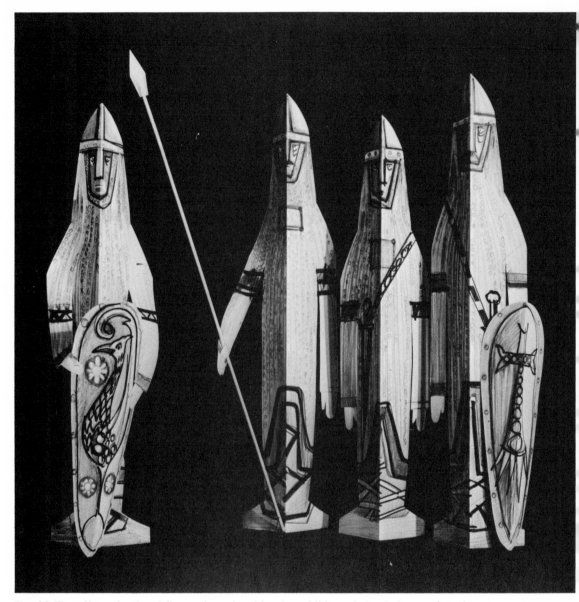

Fig. 22 The effect of painted figures is assisted by the addition of simple items of equipment.

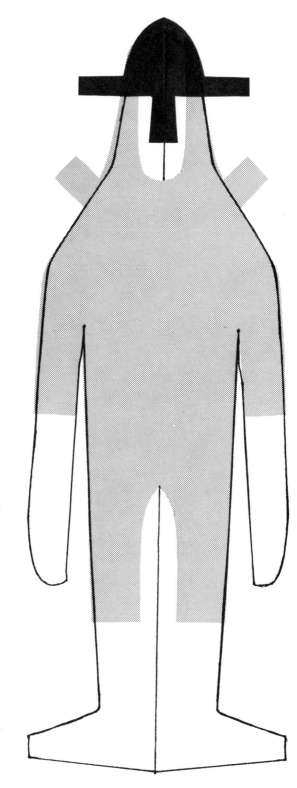

Fig. 23 Dressing the Standing
Figures is a simple matter of cutting shapes to fit.

D

You can help yourself further in making models as simple as this if you research fully enough, so that you can add important items of equipment to the figures. The shields in the illustration are an example of this. You can find the authentic shape to cut—again you can use a fairly thin cardboard—and merely placing these with the figures will give them a more sculptured look. Since the arms in the basic shape have a certain possibility of movement you can make the figures hold the shields if you want. In this sort of modelling it is adequate if you gum or staple the various parts together.

Weapons of various sorts will make your models even more interesting to look at. A length of wooden dowel or thin cane will easily convert to spears, or even a length of tightly rolled paper secured with transparent adhesive tape.

A more ambitious version of this figure might have simple added clothes. These can be cut from paper and secured with tabs behind the figures. A helmet with flaps at the side which can be folded and secured behind the head can be an optional addition. These or any other garments can be worked out at first as patterns in newspaper.

When you are evolving a pattern for a garment it might require several attempts before you can get it exactly right. The method is, however, fairly simple.

When you have the cut basic shape you can place this flat on a folded newspaper. You can draw round the shape and then add the tabs which you will need to fix the garment. You can also cut away any special parts where the garment should be shaped.

This is illustrated in the diagram (Fig. 23). The basic shape is related to the garment it will wear, and to the helmet which will go over the garment.

These additions to the basic shape which has only a graphic treatment will add a quality to your work with the free-standing figures (Fig. 24). They will give them more form, since every additional piece will add slightly to the over-all dimensions.

The version of the Roman soldiers (Fig. 25) further illustrates the way in which the basic shape can be built up. In this instance the uniforms are added without a centre fold. They can be cut in this way

Fig. 24 Simple paper costumes will add form to the Single-Fold Figures.

Fig. 25 The Single-Fold Figures can be developed by using reference works for simple costume details.

if a pattern is first made and then placed flat on the paper for the uniforms. The effect of this is to make the dressed figures appear even rounder, although they are still developments of a basic shape.

In this example, if you look closely you will see that extra flaps have been left at the ankles when the basic shapes have been cut. These have been turned and fixed at the back to give the figures extra support. It is a useful technique when the figures are being made fairly large.

These figures also have feet added. They can be made from small pieces of cardboard folded and stuck behind the basic shape.

There are a number of variations or refinements which you can include in, or add to your basic shape. You can try any additional features which might seem to improve the appearance or stability of the standing figures. The basic shape is intended only as a point of departure. When you have understood the need for this as something to work on you are free to develop the figures as you like.

Single-fold Kings
There was a time when children had to learn the dates of Kings and Queens, which probably as much as anything tended to give History a bad name among those who had to learn it. It is possible now, of course, to spend more time thinking about the way they lived and the things they did, and especially what they looked like and the way they dressed.

The diagram (Fig. 26) illustrates simple cut paper additions which are possible to the features of a basic shape. The crown is just a simple typical shape with tabs at the side for turning to the back.

The addition of a beard and moustache will require no particular skill. They can be cut from coloured paper and stuck to the basic shape. A nose with eyebrows can also be added.

You can if you prefer draw the nose and beard, like the first example in the illustration (Fig. 27). But an added nose, with form at the centre fold, and with simple brows, will make eye sockets with shadows. This will tend to make your figures even more effective, especially from a distance.

In the diagram the nose and brow addition is illustrated with a flap which can be inserted into a slot cut in the basic shape. This is a good method of joining one feature of a model to another, and is a technique which you can include in your developing skill.

Fig. 26 Additions to the basic shape may be stuck, cut with flaps and slotted, or turned and fixed at the back.

When you are working you must learn to anticipate where you might require a flap, and must include it in your pattern-making stage. Once you have the flap ready for insertion you can hold the whole piece in position against the shape where it is to be fixed and can make marks for the slots. It is useful to do this with the point of a pin rather than with a pencil because you then get a very precise definition of the slot.

Where shapes are very simple, like the moustache, it is hardly necessary to go to the bother of including a flap, since the shape can be stuck direct with a strong adhesive. A point to remember about flaps and slots is that they do result in invisible fixtures. The flaps can be inserted and stuck out of sight at the back of the model.

In the illustration of the Kings (Fig. 27) there are three different treatments of the basic shape.

Fig. 27 Decoration of the shape may be painted, added in paper or cut from cloth.

The first is cut as a basic shape with crown included and is entirely painted. This treatment, which might appear to be the simplest, does in fact require more skill than the treatment of the other two shapes. If you do not draw particularly well this should certainly be the one you should choose last.

The second shape is treated with the additional features as in the diagram, and is dressed in paper clothes. A simple garment (Fig. 28) can form the basis for a richly patterned collar and cuffs. You should not find it difficult to make this sufficiently regal. A sword can be cut from cardboard and fixed with a belt round the figure.

The third figure is basically the same, but in this example the clothes are cut from felt and stuck to the shape. No sewing is necessary, although there is no rule which says you must not sew if you want to. Nor is there any rule which says that the basic shapes must be dressed in any particular way. You can of course use any material you like, even mixing paper and felts or other materials on the same figures.

You can also, as in previous exercises, use wool or string for the beards. You can use silver or gold foil for crowns and jewellery, and any other suitable materials which you have in the collection you should be beginning to make.

If you have a box of offcuts and decorative pieces you will add enormously to the visual effect you can make with the figures, although in the case of all materials you must experiment to find the right adhesive. The one you want is the one which will stick without staining. There are so many different branded adhesives on sale today that you must make a point of reading the instructions on the packet, or asking the retailer, before you buy any one of them.

From the figures described you should be able to see that many types of historical exercises are possible with dressed and standing figures. The simple single-fold figure can be developed into quite skilled examples of modelling. The basic shape has an almost unlimited potential.

It is necessary to use some imagination and to take some care. Your work, for example, should be as neat

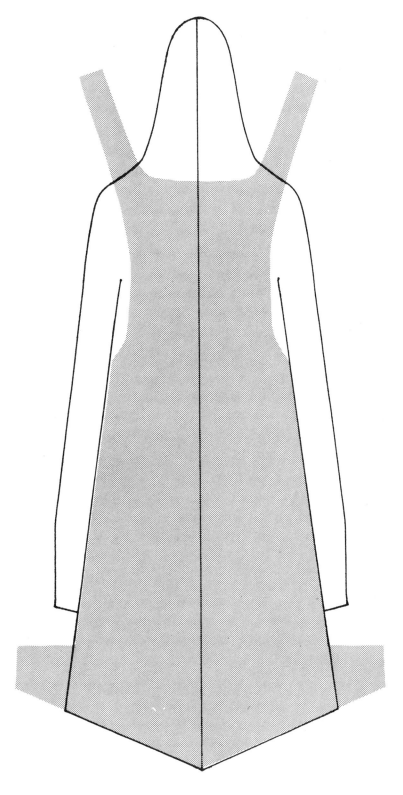

Fig. 28 Costume patterns can be cut to fit the basic shape, and should include tabs for fixing.

48   as possible and should be free from unattractive stains and blobs of glue. But this is a question of organization and practice. If you organize a special place for gluing, with plenty of newspaper to work on, you will not get it all over the working surface and consequently all over the model. If you glue something on the newspaper surface you should make sure that the next piece you glue is in a clean place or on a clean sheet.

In any craft the system you work to is important. You should try to keep a clean and uncluttered area immediately in front of you, and you should try to have a specific place for each item of equipment or material. This is a disciplined organization which is the accompaniment to skill in a craft.

Imagination in the craft is the ability to introduce effective personal touches. In the case of the figures from history, flags and banners might make colourful additions to any group—especially of knights or soldiers. The decorations on shields were sometimes deliberately made for effect, and if you are making them it might be worth spending a little time researching the decorative styles of the period. There are many reference books you can turn to, and museums where you can sometimes see actual examples. There is no doubt that if you are working seriously yourself you will find the people who are employed in these places only too willing to help in your research.

Table Figures

There are other opportunities in the use of the single-fold figures which you might investigate. You might have decided on some already, and you might have made them so that they are already being seen by other people. It is interesting to wonder how much they are really seeing, whether they are seeing characters from history or whether they see the models first as pieces of paper stuck together.

In the illustration (Fig. 29) there are a number of free-standing figures, simply cut on the fold. They are made from cardboard and some of them have slight additions to the basic shape. This might be an opportunity for you to examine the way in which you actually see things.

Fig. 29 Free-standing figures may be used in various unexpected ways.

You should look closely at the illustration to see if you can make anything special of it. When you have looked you can read the following list:

The figures are all clowns.

They start small at the left of the illustration and get progressively taller to the right.

They all have a simple check pattern on their trousers.

The pattern is in every case four squares wide.

The first clown has one lot of four.

The second, slightly taller, has two lots.

The third, slightly taller again, has three lots.

In fact they grow progressively by the addition each time of one row of four squares. Although the figures are a bit of fun, they are a graphic representation—using the single fold technique—of something quite serious, a multiplication table. From the left: once four is four, two fours are eight, and so on to the last clown who has forty-eight squares on his trousers.

There might be some of you reading this who have never been subjected to the process of having to learn multiplication tables, either the one illustrated or any of the others. These readers can go on quite happily to the next section and can leave this one alone.

But for those of you who might have to learn multiplication tables, the single-fold figure is offered as a light-hearted aid to what is sometimes a very laborious process.

Making rows of figures like this will not of course teach you a table, but you might enjoy trying to remember the answers to the multiplication of any two numbers.

You could do an exercise like this with any of the tables, but to make it work you must evolve a simple system. The squares in the example illustrated are exactly the width of a ruler. Therefore the rectangles from which the shapes are cut start by being equal to four widths of the ruler.

The height of the smallest clown is equal to one width of the ruler plus an appropriate body size; the second clown—two widths of the ruler plus the appropriate body size again. The tallest clown will be equal in height to twelve times the width of the ruler plus the body size. If you happen to be learning a table at school you might suggest doing an exercise like this to your teacher. You could explain the method, and you might work with some of your friends. It could be rather a lot of work for one person.

If you are trying to learn a table at home you might invite a friend in to help, and afterwards arrange the figures in your room so that in quiet moments you could help yourself with the learning.

There are other ways in which you might develop different groups of Table Figures. The taller figure carrying the boxes (Fig. 30) says something different about numbers. Instead of a table of clowns with check trousers you might have one of porters carrying boxes.

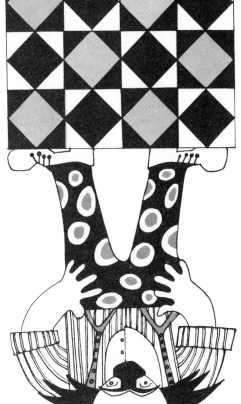

The juggler balancing a decorated prop on his feet might communicate something about three rows of four squares. In this example the message is less obvious. It is in the form of a visual code. There are three rows of four squares, and inside these—three rows of four squares again. This might be a more subtle example of the table figure. It might be interesting to try this one on your friends. It might make them think. Or better still, it might make them look. How may squares are there actually in the example shown?

This is an instance of one of the marvellous things about making and decorating things. We have to look as we work, and it helps us to see. In this way we will come to enjoy and understand more and more of the world in which we live.

The Table Figures illustrated are only some of the possible examples you might make. As alternatives you might have:

Clowns with check coats.

Knights with squared decorations on their shields.

Motherly-looking ladies with check pinafores or aprons.

A face looking over a wall of square bricks.

There are many other ideas you might introduce in order to make your work more lively. If you embark on a row of ladies wearing aprons they might have flowered patterns instead of checks. You could make a simple potato-cut to print these with, instead of having to make ruled lines and to paint each square. As long as you get the right number of flowers in each row, and the right number of rows on each figure, it will not matter how you produce them.

A measure of accuracy is of course necessary, because you are investigating another way of saying something which is accurate. If you lose the accuracy somewhere the figures will only confuse you, instead of helping you learn. And you can be sure that someone will readily point out any mistakes you make.

If your figures are accurate, however, you could have a lot of fun helping yourself learn something, which, you might already know, can at times become very tiresome.

Single-fold Christmas Figure

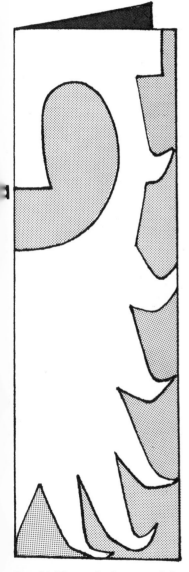

Fig. 31 The main feature of the Christmas figure can be cut in white paper.

There are occasions each year when a special standing figure might be useful. The Santa Claus figure is an obvious one, and this can be developed like previous figures on the simple basic shape.

You can start by cutting a triangular shape, preferably a tall triangle, from a rectangle of red paper or card. This can be cut on the centre fold so that it will stand without added support.

From a piece of white paper, related in size to the triangle, you can cut a simple nose and beard shape in one piece. This is illustrated in the diagram (Fig. 31), in which the shaded portions are the parts to be removed.

If you look at the diagram carefully you will see that the cut at *a* into the fold will establish the bottom of the nose. The rest of the face can be established by the curved continuation of this cut, which returns to the fold at a point under *a*.

The effect of a cut like this is illustrated in the first figure (Fig. 32). There are no eyes or other features on this figure, but you should be able to see that when the white paper is opened out against the darker background it begins to suggest the Christmas figure. Before opening the paper you will, of course, have cut the beard-like shape at the edges.

The second figure is developed more fully. It has simple eyes and a moustache. It also has arms which can be cut separately—they can be slightly curved—and can be stuck behind the body. These arms can have cut hands, and the figures can have other simple decorative features, like the large button or the white band at the bottom of the body.

If you want to curl the points of the whiskers as in the illustration you must use the paper sculptor's technique. You must hold the base of each point carefully so that you will not tear it away from the main paper, and you must run a scissor or knife blade along the length of the piece to be curled. The easiest way to do this is to hold the paper at the base of the point in one hand. Holding the blade in the other hand you can run it along the bottom of the strip with your thumb at the top. The movement should start at the base and run off the paper at the tip.

This action should disturb the tension on one side

Fig. 32 The Christmas figure may be simple, or it may be developed with added features.

of the paper, causing it to spring into a neat curl. It is probably a technique which you will need to practise on strips of paper before you actually try it on the figure. But you should be able to learn it quickly. It is a question of getting the feel of it, so that you are neither too brutal nor too tentative.

Various other single-fold figures can be made on any theme or subject which interests you. If you are doing a particular project at school; it might be a study of the environment or a geographical study of a foreign country, you could research and make the appropriate types of figure.

You might make some of your favourite figures from fiction, or other personalities whose image appeals to you. You can, in fact, make any figure. If you make it with a vertical fold through the centre it should stand up. There is always a shelf or a corner in a room somewhere which has space for an interesting and carefully-made figure.

Single-fold Mounted Figures

When you are making figures as historical illustrations you will find it useful to develop a way of making the figures mounted. The horse was an essential part of the general equipment in many periods of history.

It is not a difficult step from the free-standing figures of the previous exercises to a simple type of figure which, although based on the same principle, can be made to sit astride a model horse.

In the diagram (Fig. 33) the same basic shape as you used previously is shown with variations at the feet and legs.

The feet should be drawn as illustrated, pointing to the centre fold. They should be cut at this point *a*, so that they will not be joined when the shape is opened. The shaded portions in the diagram will be removed by the cutting.

The feet and legs cut this way will point forward when the shape is opened so that it can be made to sit astride a horse (Fig. 36).

Horses can be made in various ways. A simple

E

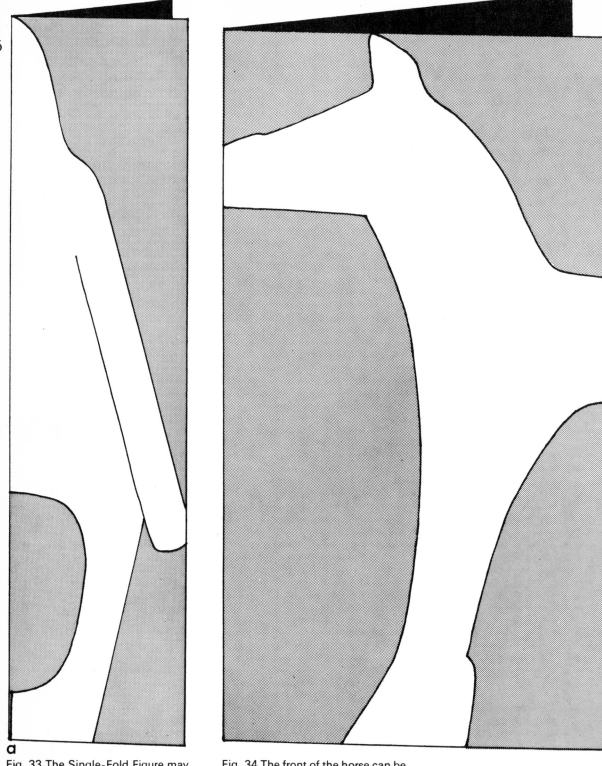

a

Fig. 33 The Single-Fold Figure may
be developed so that it can become
a mounted figure.

Fig. 34 The front of the horse can be
cut double with a join at the muzzle.

method is illustrated in the diagrams (Figs. 34–36).

To start with you will need a cardboard cylinder. You can make this yourself with rolled and stuck cardboard, or you can use a toilet roll or kitchen towel centre.

For the front part of the horse you can cut a head and legs in one piece (Fig. 34). This must be cut from doubled cardboard, so that the horse has two sides. You will see from the diagram that the front of the muzzle is joined at the fold. The two pieces are not separate. They must remain joined at this point.

The rear portion of the horse can be cut in the same way, with the legs as appropriately shaped as possible (Fig. 35). The two rear legs are also cut as one piece, and must remain joined at the top.

Fig. 35 The back legs of the horse can also be cut as a double shape, although the legs must be separate.

Fig. 36 The front and back shapes
can be assembled on a card cylinder
as a mount for the figure.

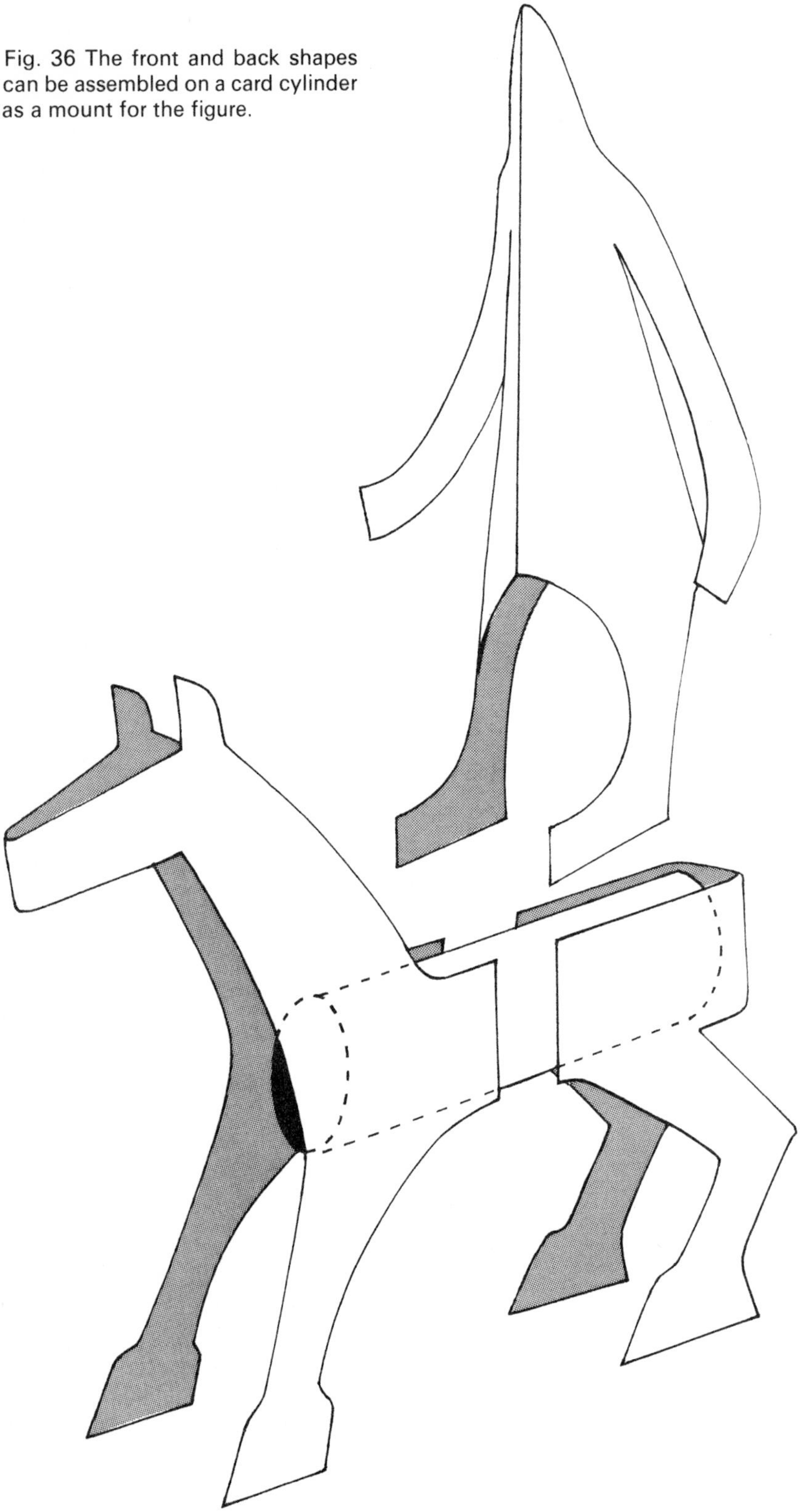

Fig. 37 The mounted figures can be dressed simply and can be developed with various decorative treatments.

The front and rear sections of the horse can be assembled on the cylinder either by stapling, or with pierce-through paper-fasteners which can be opened on the inside of the cylinder. The positioning for assembly is illustrated (Fig. 36).

If the legs are not strong enough after assembly to support the body and the rider they can be gently scored along their length, from hoof to top, and slightly folded. You will remember from previous exercises that a fold will introduce added strength into paper and cardboard.

Dressing the figures and horses can be done in the same way as previous exercises. This is at this stage a basic shape for you to work on. You must again use reference sources as a guide, and you must keep the models as simple as possible.

The figures in the illustration (Fig. 37) are dressed

in paper clothes. They are intended to represent mounted versions of the Norman soldiers which were illustrated in an earlier exercise.

In this case they are dressed in a basic tunic or hauberk, a coat of chain mail. It will help, if you want to make something like this, to think of the shape it would be if you had to wear such a garment yourself. You will again have to work out a pattern in paper before cutting the final version for the model, and you must remember that the figure this time is going to be seated astride the horse. You can see the cut-away part of the hauberk in the front figure.

A hood for the hauberk can be cut separately to give a dramatic protective appearance, with an opening for the face. In this sort of modelling a measure of authenticity is desirable, but the general effect can be more important than detailed accuracy. In this case the intention is to give the figures a protected and business-like look, and a certain liberty has been taken with the shape and size of the hood.

The figures can be made more effective visually if the parts which represent armour can be sprayed with a silver or metallic paint. It is possible to buy this quite inexpensively in a spray canister. The smallest size will last for a long time, since a satisfactory armour effect can be made with only one coat of spray over paper or cloth.

If you are going to use a spray you must take some care to use it properly. In the first place you must read the manufacturer's directions. You must also make your own simple version of the professional's spray booth. You should preferably spray your models out of doors, either against a newspaper backing or inside a cardboard carton placed on its side.

If you buy a silver spray you will find it useful for many historical figures, but you must remember to turn it upside-down after use and clear the jet, otherwise it will be useless for later exercises.

Shields and weapons for the mounted figures can also be made to look reasonably authentic. These are fun to make and they add enormously to what are really very simple versions of the original.

To develop and decorate the horses you will be able to make a simple paper covering or caparison. This can be plain with the minimum of painted decoration, as in the first figure, or it can be cut with a more decorative edge shape. It can be stapled or stuck to the horse.

After cutting and fixing the caparison you might like to add a tail or mane. This can be made with paper, or with wool or string, and can be stuck to the cardboard shape with an instant glue. You can also add wool or string to the fetlocks in order to make the legs slightly more substantial in appearance.

If you are working on a suitable period of history at school you might make some mounted figures with a group of friends. You can again decorate them with banners and pennants, and can find a convenient shelf or window-sill on which to display them.

Although these are basic shapes which can be made almost entirely in cardboard and paper, a group displayed together will make an impressive exhibition. Both the figures and the horses can, of course, be developed to illustrate any period of history. There are suggestions for different sorts of armour in later exercises, but the basic shape demonstrated should be strong enough for you to develop and dress it in any way you like.

Cylinder Figures

At this point in your work, if you are following some of the suggested exercises, you will be making sculptured forms. It should be possible already for you to display examples of your work so that they can be viewed from any angle. They are three-dimensional.

Your mounted figures in the previous exercise might have been planned mainly from the front, but you might have felt it necessary as you worked to finish them off neatly at the back. This would imply that you are already getting a feeling for form in three dimensions; and you are ready, when you reach this stage, to consider in more detail the real potential of the papers and cardboard you are using. If you can begin to understand and appreciate this potential you will begin to be very much in control of the craft.

A sheet of paper is two-dimensional. It has height and it has width, but it has no depth. In a drawing on the sheet, depth has to be communicated by means of a trick. The artist must use shading or tone, or he must draw in perspective.

But a sheet of paper does have a three-dimensional potential. It can be manipulated into certain forms.

You have seen that a single fold introduced as a vertical into a piece of paper will give it a type of form on the two planes which join at the fold. This is a useful shape for modelling on, but it is limited. It is not really an all-round free-standing shape.

Shapes with these qualities can, however, be developed in paper. You can investigate this simply for yourself by taking any sheet of paper. A sheet of typing paper would be a convenient size.

You can look at this sheet and search for the simplest all-round shape you can make with it, which will stand freely and unsupported. This will probably be a roll or a cylinder if you start with a rectangle.

The cylinder can be raised from any flat square or rectangle of paper. It can be fixed at the point of overlap by gumming or stapling. It can be narrow in diameter, or it can be wide so that there is only a minimal overlap for fixing. When you have raised this form it is three-dimensional, and if you have been careful it will stand freely without leaning or toppling over.

This is a basic shape. The material you are using throughout these exercises can be constructed into this form, which can be used as the basis for many sculptural developments.

If your first cylinder is plain, it would be easy to put two eyes and a nose on it. This would immediately give it some identity, and instead of being merely a cylinder the paper would have become a simple sculptured head.

You could, if you liked, add hair and ears or any other relevant features, which would be another act of modelling on a basic form. You would put the eyes and nose on what you had decided was to be the front of the cylinder, and you would have arranged the hair at the back. You could do all this again in many different ways—with different colours, different features and different placing of the parts. The basic shape has an unlimited potential. It can be exploited in any way you like.

Skittle Figures

You are not looking for a ponderous or highly important way of working on the basic cylinder. You will have realized that paper and cardboard offer opportunities for fun. They are not materials which will last for ages. They are cheap and gay and easily replaced, and although you should be prepared to spend a certain amount of time working with them, nothing you do should be excessively demanding in time or industry.

The history models which you made earlier might have been fun, but there was a serious aspect to that work. Now you can play with the basic shape.

The skittles (Fig. 38) are cylinders of paper, developed as figures with simple cut-out arm shapes. You can make these added shapes by folding a second piece of paper, suitably smaller than the cylinder, and cutting the corners so that it will become a circular or oval shape. The centre can be cut from this so that when it is placed against the cylinder it will suggest arms behind the figure's back.

This shape will only suggest arms. It will not define or describe them exactly. It suggests them because it makes a simple statement of the obvious. If you place the additions at the backs of the figures you will not expect them to suggest legs. Although they are very simple, they are obviously where the arms should be, and as such we can accept them for what is intended.

There are ways, of course, of adding more realistic arms to the cylinders. If you prefer you can work out a method of your own. In this case the arms are kept very simple because instead of standing as though ready to do something, the figures are intended to stand as though waiting patiently to be bowled over.

There are various decorative treatments which can be used on the skittles. Like other exercises they can be painted or coloured with crayons, or they can be dressed with decorative papers like the blonde lady in the illustration. The decorative treatment, painted or stuck, can be applied before the cylinder is made up. This can be done with the face also if it is found to be an easier method than working on the made-up form.

The moustache on the male figure is a deliberate exaggeration. It is an illustration of the way in which

Fig. 38 Skittles can be developed on a basic shape, and can be painted or developed with patterned papers

a simple but visually dramatic effect can be achieved by stretching reality a little to suit yourself. This is one of the great pleasures of working in art and craft. There is no rule which says you have to conform. No one will say to you that in any work you have done something is not like the real thing, or is not exactly as it ought to be.

If they do you must just humour them with a tolerant smile, while you reflect on all the fun they are probably missing.

If you make a group of these skittles you can really play with them although they are made in paper. You could set them up somewhere in the house, giving each of them a number. You could then take it in turns with friends to roll a ball along the ground, trying to score by knocking them over. If you place the skittles carefully, with gaps between them slightly

wider than the ball, you will make the game interesting, and will probably be surprised to discover how easy it is to miss the figures when you bowl. If you or your friends bowl too fiercely, of course, you will soon ruin the skittles. If you want to make a fast game of it you must begin by making them with cardboard cylinders.

When you are able to make colourful and amusing examples of the skittles, you might suggest a game to your teacher. If you could persuade him to let you play skittles in the classroom you might justify it by using the opportunity to support some of your work. It might be a way, for example, of developing some quick calculations. If you were at that particular time working with fractions, you could label each skittle with a number which included a fraction. You could then take turns at bowling, and the number of skittles each of you knocked over would make interesting calculations as you worked out each player's score. This might be an unusual form of mathematics to find in school, and it might not be expected to teach you very much. But it would liven up your mental arithmetic exercises, and you could always let your teacher have a turn.

Supporters The skittle figures can be used in many other ways. If you are interested in football and have a favourite team, or in any other game, you might make some supporters on the basic cylinder. In an earlier exercise there was a reference to games and players, which you could now develop on this form. But the cylinder is probably more suited for supporters than for players.

You could make some of these, if you were interested, wearing scarves and hats in your team's colours. They could be painted both sides. On one side they could be smiling and cheerful (Fig. 39), and they could be set up this way round when your team won a match.

On the back of the same figures you could paint them looking dejected and thoroughly fed-up. You could turn them this way round when your team lost a match (Fig. 40).

66

Fig. 39 Various types of figure can be developed on the basic shape, supporting a football team for example.

Fig. 40 The figures can be made reversible.

These figures could make a decoration for your room, or again you could persuade your teacher to let you make them with a group of friends in school. If you had them on show in the classroom during the season, you might be early on the mornings after your team had won in order to turn the smiling faces forward. If they lost you would probably find that some of your school friends, supporters of other teams, would have turned them with the bleak faces outwards before you arrived.

If you are not interested in football as a reason for smiling or scowling, you might be interested in making figures which would respond to some other sort of situation.

In a classroom you could have figures able to smile or scowl according to the weather. This could be a light-hearted variation on the weather charts which many of you will already have in your classrooms.

If you are in a school which has a competitive system of marks you could have figures which would respond to your class or team progress—or lack of it— throughout the term.

There must be some activity which either saddens or pleases you according to its progress, and which might provide you with a reason for making some Supporters.

Prism Figures

The cylinder which you have been working with is only one of the basic shapes on which you can develop three-dimensional work with paper. This has now become a basic skill in your technique, and you should be able to rely on it as a foundation for a variety of modelled forms—either faces or figures.

Although the cylinder, being a basic shape, will be common to anyone working in the craft, it will always be personal in style according to the person using it. This will also apply to other basic shapes.

If you take another rectangle of paper, similar to the one from which you made your first cylinder, you can raise a form in it by making it into a prism. In order to do this, instead of rolling the paper, you will have to fold it so that it has sides of equal size.

The simplest example of this is the triangular prism.

To make a triangular prism from the rectangle you should place it flat on the working surface, with the longer sides horizontal.

Your first fold should be at the side, establishing the strip or 'seam' for sticking the raised form. The width of this seam should relate to the height of the prism you are making. If this is going to be very tall the seam must be adequately wide. For normal-sized work a seam about the width of a ruler should be adequate.

After folding the seam you must fold the remaining paper longways into three equal strips. You can find a method of doing this by overlapping the sections, or if you prefer to be more accurate you can use a ruler, measuring the strip at the top and bottom. For a triangular prism you will have two folds, with a third fold making the seam.

When you make up the form it will have three faces. Where the cylinder has a circular shape at the top and bottom, the triangular prism will have shapes with three sides, or triangles. Like the cylinder it should stand freely without leaning or toppling over.

This is another basic shape on which you can work. To develop a face on this you can choose, as the front, one of the planes or you can establish the front at one of the folding points. The difference in visual effect can be interesting.

Standing figures can be treated in the same way. They can have arms added, and can be dressed or decorated to suit any theme you are working on.

This triangular prism is another basic shape which you can include in the range of techniques you are developing. It is strong enough to model on, and will support various figure developments.

If you can understand and construct the triangular prism, it should be a simple matter for you to work out the construction of the square and rectangular prisms. It should be obvious that the square prism will have a square at its top and base, and that this can be varied to a rectangle with the rectangular prism. There are other factors which you will understand. Both of the prisms will, for example, be four-sided. In the case of the square prism the sides will be equal, that is all four of them. But with the rectangular prism only the opposite sides will be equal.

If you look around your house you will be able to see cardboard prisms of various sorts. You will probably find the best collection of these in the kitchen. What sort of shape is the box which holds your breakfast cereal?

When you see square or rectangular prism shapes in use they are unlikely, of course, to have open ends like those you might make as basic shapes from flat paper. But when you are using prisms for figures you are unlikely to need the ends enclosed. If you do want to close the ends you must make an endpiece the same size as the prism, and you must include flaps as sticking seams.

When you have included the prism shapes in your technique you can investigate opportunities for developing them. It is not necessary to find a way immediately of using all the different shapes. They are in reserve for any occasion in the future when you might need another basic form on which to work.

An example of the way in which the prism may be developed is illustrated (Fig. 41). These faces are open-ended and are made up from rectangles of the same size. When you first look at the illustration you will probably, since you should be thinking about the technique, see a number of faces made on tall square prisms.

This is so, but there is an added feature. If you look more closely you will see that all the faces have the same-shaped nose. They were cut in one operation from folded paper. It is interesting to see how a different placing of the same shape will alter the final effect, and how it is not necessary all the time to search for change and originality.

This is another exercise you might try at home, or you might suggest to your teacher. Making the prisms might be a good exercise in accurate measuring and practice in the use of the ruler. If a group of you make a number of faces you could place them in this sort of pyramid formation on the classroom window sill. The rows can be supported on each other with strips of card cut slightly wider than the prisms.

If you have a sympathetic teacher and a suitable

Fig. 41 Different basic shapes will provide new opportunities for figure development.

classroom you could set up a number of Prism Figures in an arrangement similar to the illustration, and using balls of compressed newspaper could take turns to see how many you can knock down—a fair in the classroom. It is a quick and quite demanding exercise in mental arithmetic if the figures are numbered—for example: score one for the top row, two for the middle and three for the bottom row—and if all you knock down have to be multiplied together. What would be the score if you knocked them all down?

It is obvious that you could not expect your teacher to allow you to do something like this every day, but there must be moments during the week when you all —pupils and teacher—would be glad of a less serious diversion, if only for a few minutes. It is better if the subject for such a diversion can be things which you have made yourselves.

The square prisms which are illustrated are of course not for you to copy. They have been made up with a simple and precise treatment so that the illustration will be clear to the reader. If you are making prisms you can employ any sort of decorative treatment.

Like the cylinders the prisms can be finished flat, and then raised as forms, if you find this method easier than working with them upright.

With any of your work on basic forms you will realize that they are intended to be free-standing. If you make a lot, however, you might run out of shelf space. In which case they can be pinned to the wall instead of standing. Treated in this way they will become examples of low relief rather than three-dimensional sculpture, but they will still retain and show some of the form which you made by using the technique of folding from the flat to a basic shape.

Figure Forms

The basic shapes which you have been investigating, and on which you have been modelling faces and figures, are suitable for a large variety of occasions. They are a valuable addition to your developing skill and should support your work as you evolve a personal style.

Style is the way you will select and draw and cut. It is what will make your work different from the illustrations or from the work of anyone else. Your style will in fact disguise the basic forms.

The next stage is to develop your own forms for specific instances of figure modelling. These will not be better than the basic shapes. They will be opportunities for you to manipulate your paper or card deliberately so that it will serve you exactly as you want it to, and will extend your ability to model with the material.

With the experience you already have you might now look at the form of the human figure and interpret it in other ways in cardboard.

If you begin with a strip of cardboard and the idea that you want to make a standing figure, you can simplify your requirements. The figure must stand, therefore you need a base. The figure must be three-dimensional, therefore you need a back and front. Can you make the strip meet this specification? You are unlikely to be able to do this entirely. But you could fold a base in the middle of the strip, raising the two sides and making them meet at the top.

This is illustrated in the diagram (Fig. 42). It is a fairly complex diagram at first glance, but if you read it carefully it is no more complicated than any of the others you have already used.

In the first instance you should read the diagram, ignoring the toned area at the bottom which is enclosed with a dotted line. This is included for a later development of the shape.

The diagram shows a long strip of paper—preferably of good stiff quality—or thin cardboard folded vertically through its centre. The vertical fold will be at the centre of the figure, so it is the area of the diagram nearer the fold in which you should be interested.

This area is divided into three sections. At the top there is an extended cone shape, with rounded top—and with an arm. This will be the back upright of the figure.

Immediately below this is the area which will form the base on which the figure will stand. When the shape is cut out and opened it must be folded across its width at *aa*, and again at *bb*.

The lowest section is a similar cone shape to that at the top, but instead of arms it has simple flaps or tabs which will be used for fixing the raised form. Ignore the toned area at this stage.

The illustration (Fig. 43) shows how this shape can be raised to make a deliberate figure form. This is essentially different from any of the previous basic forms. It is a specific figure. If you wanted, any of the previous forms could be developed as shapes which were not human. If you cut a lot of hair and used a suitable colour, yellow for example, you could develop the cylinder as a lion. With ears and a tail and the right-shaped face it could be a simple cat.

The shape illustrated (Fig. 43) has been deliberately developed to meet the specified standing figure requirement. The arms, which are included on the back of the form, may be bent forward as in the illustration. The flaps which were included on the front section can be folded at the back and secured. It is a simple figure, which can now be dressed and treated in various ways.

If you try to make a shape like this it is quite reasonable for you to follow this diagram and the directions closely. This is a shape which has been arrived at after considerable experiment, and it is one which can be used over and over again, and by anybody. The illustrations which immediately follow this exercise show ways in which the form can be developed, but these are only a few of the many different possibilities. It is a useful form on which to model figures because it is both strong and versatile. It can be used as a standing figure. It can also be used for hanging figures or for decorative figures which will be pinned to a wall.

The form is developed in the illustration of the Three Kings (Fig. 44). Like the kings in earlier exercises these have added noses and whiskers, and the basic forms are dressed with plain and patterned papers.

The contrast between the patterned paper and the plain in each figure tends to make the use of the pattern more effective by concentrating it in a particular part of the form. This is a small but useful point to remember in decoration. If you are going to use brightly

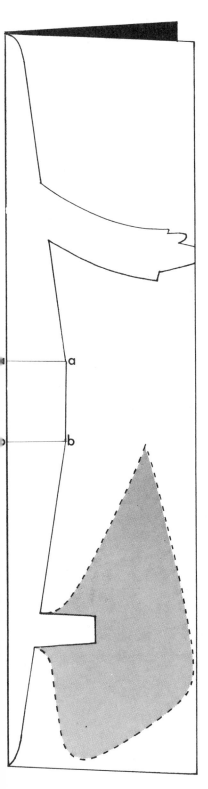

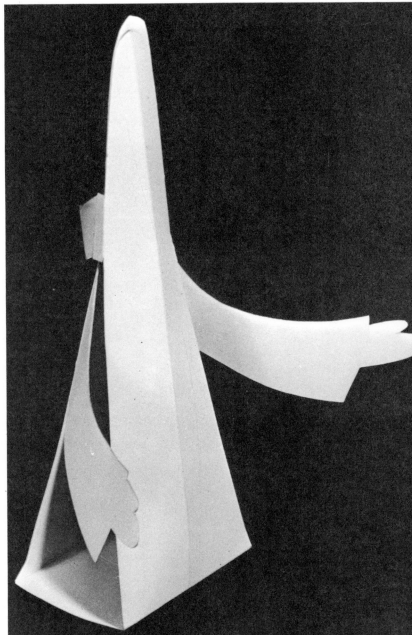

Fig. 43 The Figure Form will be free-standing when the flaps are joined.

Fig. 42 A Figure Form can be raised on parallel folds at the centre of the shape.

Fig. 44 Contrast between plain and patterned papers will add to the decorative effect of finished models.

coloured and exciting patterns, it is sometimes an advantage to limit the pattern effect and to support it with a balance of plain colour.

The plain colour may be related to any dominant colour in the pattern. It may echo it or it may contrast with it. You can see this in the black and silver striped pattern which is echoed in the black cloak of the figure on the right of the illustration.

There is again no rule which has to be followed, but you should try to be aware of the effect of contrast and support as you work. You should look as closely as you can at your work, trying to make deliberate decisions about colour and pattern. Of course you can experiment and enjoy yourself. But you should look at the visual effect all the time, and as often as possible you should think about it and relate it to other effects which, from earlier experience, you know to be possible.

The contrast effect in the group of Kings has been included deliberately. It is not the only way to dress the Kings for a Nativity group. The simple fur collar cut in paper and slightly curled is a useful technique for a rich effect, as is the use of gold or silver-faced cardboard. For the Kings the quality of richness is the one you will want to achieve.

If you were to use the basic figure form for the development of other figures in a Nativity group you would need to consider other qualities.

The shepherds, for example, could be covered in a similar way by sticking papers over the basic form, but the rich decorative papers would have to be kept for the kings. For the shepherds you would need plain colours, with perhaps a simple band of stripes used occasionally, and with restraint, for contrast.

You could tell the Christmas story with figures like these developed in the form of a puppet show. If you make this form in thin card—4 or 8 sheet, or something of similar thickness—you will find that it has considerable upright strength. It should be possible to fix these figures at the base to narrow strips of stiff cardboard, or to thin strips of wood, so that you can push and pull them along as simple puppets from the wings of a toy stage.

You could not expect to get any sort of complex animation into the scene, but the figures could be adequately effective in themselves; and the simplest movement on to the stage could be supported with the superb text of the Christmas story.

Reference to methods of improvizing puppet stages will be found later in the sections dealing specifically with puppetry.

The figure form developed as the Nativity Kings
can be used in many different ways. It can be used for
any free-standing historical figure. You will have seen
this potential as you studied the diagram and its
development.

There is an alternative way of cutting the original
form. To understand this you must go back to the
diagram (Fig. 42), and this time you must include
the toned form at the bottom which you were asked
to ignore previously.

This pear-shaped form can now be included in the
basic shape. It will absorb, as shown, the flaps which
were previously included to make the join on the raised
form.

In the diagram the toned area stops on a level with
the line *bb*. At this point it is the lower tip of the wing
of the angel figure. If it were cut overlapping this
base line the wing would be longer than the back
of the figure, and might make standing the form
difficult.

If you cut the shape to include the wings you will
find that when the form is raised on the two base lines
aa and *bb*, the wings will be at the back of the figure
(Fig. 45). The arms must still be bent forward as they
were when the King figures were constructed. For the
angel figures a final fixture can be made at the root of
the wings, which was the fixture point in the previous
example.

In the illustrated examples various different treatments are shown. In one case the wings are cut and
slightly curled. The same technique is used in another
case, but this time it is in foil added to the surface of
the wing. On one figure the wing is decorated with a
single piece of patterned foil; on another the foil is
applied in small pieces.

For features on the angels you would really need no
more than a simple nose and brow shape cut on the
fold. Using a felt tip you could make simple dots for
the eyes and a small circle shape for the mouth. You
will probably find it difficult to paint the faces, so it
is best to use the simple formal treatment suggested.
This will in any case be in keeping with the formal
quality of the shape.

Hair can be added in paper cut in one of a number

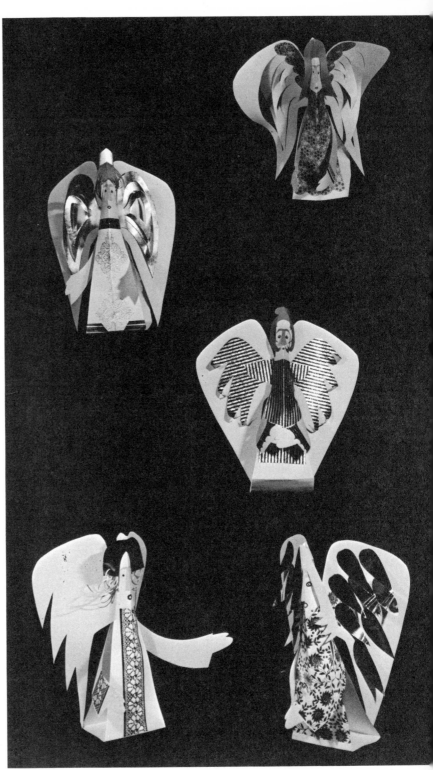

Fig. 45 Various decorative treatments can be tried with the hanging or standing angel figure.

of different ways. It can be a simple solid shape, or it can be cut in thin strands. In either case curling is possible.

The angel modelled on this figure form will demonstrate the versatility of the basic shape. As an angel it can stand freely. It can be fixed to the wall with wings outstretched, or it can be displayed hanging from a thread.

As a hanging figure it will have almost no weight. A number of them could be suspended from strings stretched across a room. They can be hung with arms open, or the hands can be joined together in a prayer-like gesture. When they are hanging they will move slowly, and this motion can be exploited if you use a small amount of foil on each form. This can be coloured and will catch the light as the figures move. It will add considerably to the effect of the decoration.

In this section you have been introduced to a number of basic forms on which it might be possible for you to model figures. If you have tried any of the examples you should have seen that they incorporate a potential which can be varied over and over again. Their further development will depend on your willingness to experiment.

Some of the forms might be used, for example, as table decorations. These could be developed as specific figures representing your guests—if you could pick out and exploit appropriate characteristics. This might be the colour or length of their hair, or the way they dress.

If this is too difficult you might make simple colourful figures, using one of the techniques, and you could let them hold labels inscribed with the names of each of your guests.

For a party you could make the figures into flower sellers. You might even arrange them to hold a few real flowers. Or you could make them serve more useful, as well as decorative, functions.

If you stapled the hands of a figure together it might make a container for drinking straws, or for paper napkins.

There are many possibilities. If you like making things, and you have time, you should now have a

Rolled Paper Figures   When you are using one of the basic forms on which
to model a figure, you are really doing no more than
making a simple body to dress. As people can dress in
different clothes you can change the appearance of the
figures. The basic forms are suitable for any dressed
treatment, and are useful parts of the skill you are
developing. But in some contexts they have the disadvantage of being very limited in movement potential.

For decorations and static displays this is of course
no disadvantage, but there might be occasions when
the lack of flexibility in the figure would make it
difficult to get the required effect.

You have seen that it is necessary to adapt the basic
form if the figure has to be mounted, but this does not
solve the problem of figures which you might want
in other positions. The most obvious difficulty is the
problem of the seated figure—a king, for example, on
a throne. This is the sort of requirement which might
often occur if you are making figures for a project in
history. You might also want figures which can demonstrate the use of farm implements or tools, or which
have to be carrying something.

It would be useful for any of these occasions to
evolve a figure form which can be more flexible for
modelling and dressing, but which at the same time
can retain the strength quality of the basic shapes.

A figure made of rolled newspaper on a wire base
or armature can be developed in many ways, and can
be made so that it has almost as much movement
potential as the human figure.

A simple method is illustrated in the diagram (Fig.
46). Before beginning the figure you should get some
newspapers in as clean and uncrumpled condition as
possible.

These can be cut into strips of equal width, preferably across the paper so that the fold at the spine is
incorporated. A suitable width for the strips is between
two and three inches, although they can be larger if
you want to model on a larger scale.

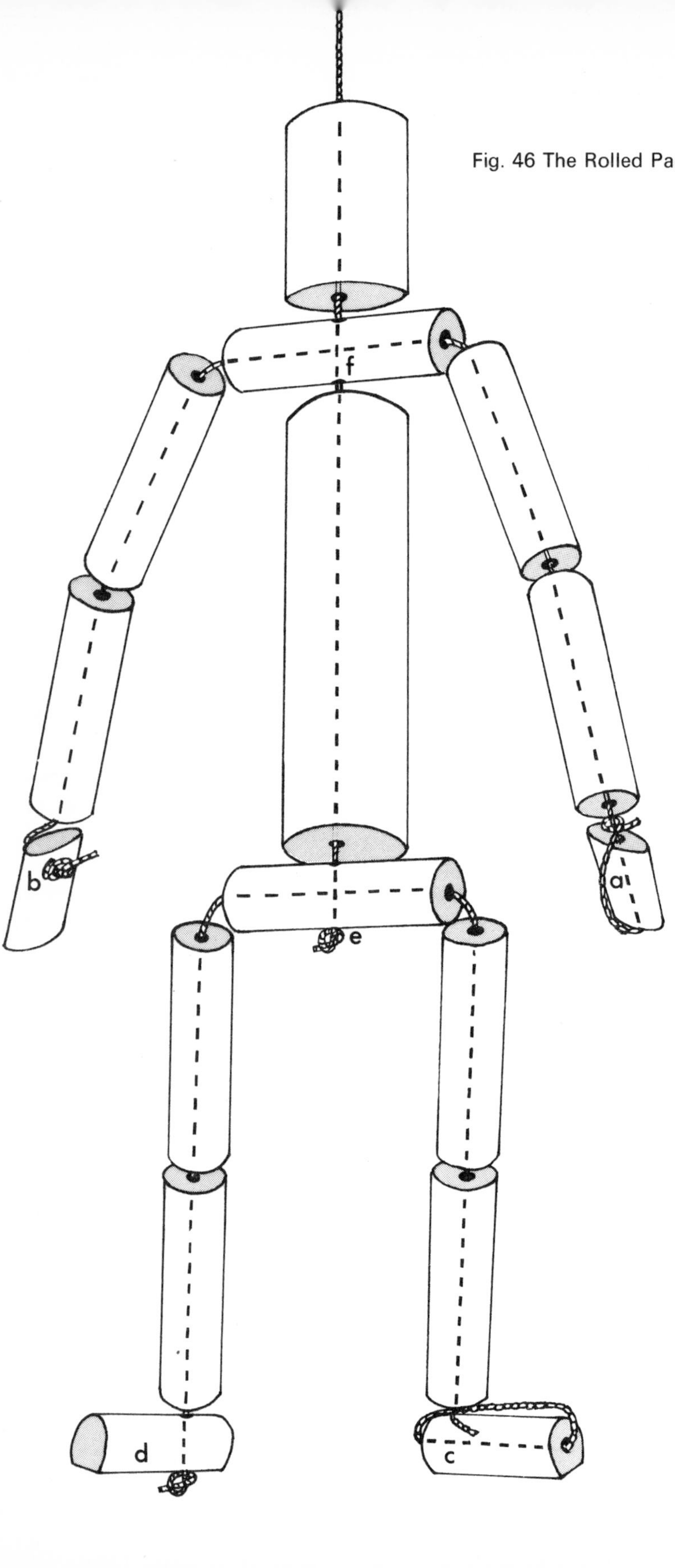

Fig. 46 The Rolled Paper figure can be made up on a wire or string base.

It should be possible to cut a number of the strips in one operation through the thickness of a newspaper. This will depend on the state of your scissors and the strength which you have in your fingers. If you have access to a paper guillotine, cutting the strips is no problem.

The cylindrical shapes in the diagram will be made from these strips rolled neatly, and then stuck with gummed tape.

For standing or modelled figures the newspaper strips should be rolled on a wire framework. This should be strong enough to support the figure, but not so thick that bending and cutting are difficult.

A coil of galvanized iron wire, which can be bought by weight in a hardware store, is likely to be the most suitable sort of wire if you are able to afford it. You can test the suitability of the gauge or thickness by bending it with your fingers. If you need pliers to bend it, it is probably too thick. Although you will need pliers, of course, to cut it.

It is often possible to find wire in a garden or tool shed. It is the sort of odd material which tends to be collected and saved. It is not important what sort of wire you can find as long as you can bend it, and as long as it will keep its shape after bending. If the only wire you can get appears to be too thin you can coil two or more strands together before using it.

The figure itself must be made up in separate sections, which can be assembled together afterwards. You should make the arm section first, and then the leg section which is made in a similar way. If you follow the directions as they are given, and refer to the diagram as you work, you should be able to learn the construction of the figure in the time it takes you to make the rolls.

Hand and Arm section

You must start with a length of wire long enough to stretch from *a* to *b*. The first fixture on the wire will be the hand at *a*. You can either make a roll round the wire, or you can begin with a hand made separately and then pierced with the end of the wire. Both methods are illustrated. The hands can be made from slightly narrower strips than the rest of the rolls, and these can be hammered flat instead of being left cylindrical.

After starting at the first hand you must continue along the wire with five separate rolls, which will make the two arms and the shoulders.

The section must be finished with the second hand *b*, and tied off so that the rolls remain on the wire.

Each roll of newspaper must be stuck after it is rolled round the wire. The simplest method is with the type of brown gummed strip which you might have used in a previous exercise. If a gummed strip is not available, ordinary transparent adhesive tape can be used.

Foot and Leg section

This section must be made in the same way as the arms. You must start at one foot *c* and, with five equal rolls in between, must tie off at the other foot *d*.

You will now have two sections complete in themselves.

The Body

A centre wire, which will act as a backbone for the figure, can be inserted into the pelvis or hip section of the legs, or if you cannot drill through the roll it can be wound round it at this point *e*.

The body section should be twice as large as any of the other individual pieces, both in thickness and in length. It must be rolled round the wire which extends upwards from the fixture at *e*.

The shoulders can now be pierced or drilled at the centre, so that the backbone wire can join the body section to the arms *f*. At this point, if drilling is not possible, the wire can be wound round the roll.

The Head

The roll for the head must be made immediately above the shoulders on the top part of the centre wire. In the case of all figures which are to be modelled, the centre wire can now be bent down at the back of the head and secured by winding at the neck.

If you have followed these stages with the help of the diagram you should now have a figure, roughly

correct in proportion, and capable of a certain amount   85
of movement at the joints.

It should be possible to make the figure stand,
although at this stage it might need a little support.
It will probably help if you can flatten the bottoms of
the feet slightly.

It should also be possible to arrange the figure in a
sitting or kneeling position, or in any other position.
It can be made to lie on its back, crouch, or stand with
arms outstretched as though holding something.

You must remember that in its final modelled form
the figure will often be depicted with something
which can act as an extra support. This might be a
shield or a spear, which the figure can be made to
hold and which will have the effect of making a
tripod at the base.

If the figure has a tendency to be weak in any particular spot, it can be strengthened with added gummed
tape. Your intention with this figure should be to make
it do exactly what you want it to. The rolls make the
basic shape, but when you have constructed the
figure you must be the craftsman in charge.

The Face
To make a simple face on the head section you can
soak some newspaper with paper-hanger's paste, so
that it becomes wet and malleable. You will only need
enough paper to make a nose and simple brow for
this figure.

When the paper is wet it can be modelled and stuck
to the head. It can be kept in position with a few overpasted pieces of tissue, which, drying with the papier
mâché, will make a permanent fixture of the features.

In later exercises you will see this method applied
in more detail to features for puppetry, but for
historical and other static models nothing very complex is necessary in the features. It is enough merely to
indicate the face.

The main effect with these figures will be realized
in the way you dress them. The clothes with their
special styles will be more important than the features,
although the modelling can be supported with a
certain amount of simple painting (Fig. 47). The use
of wool for hair, and other trimmings like jewellery,

Fig. 47 The figures can be made of newspaper but the final effect will disguise the basic construction.

will add greatly to the finished effect.

The soldiers which you have seen in previous examples of modelling are again illustrated developed on the Rolled Paper figures (Fig. 48). These have the chain-mail shirt or hauberk made from coarse hessian or burlap sprayed with silver paint. You can use an old sack for this.

Fig. 48 An old sack and a silver paint spray will make a type of chain mail possible.

The helmets are made as simple cones in cardboard with the nosepiece projecting down at the front. These, together with the spears and shields, are also sprayed silver. The shields and spears are fixed to the figures with rubber bands.

A few small circles of cardboard, cut separately and stuck to the shield and helmet before spraying, will add to the effect and will give a metallic look to these parts of the finished model.

Materials like burlap or coarse furnishing fabrics are useful for modelling figures in chain mail. They take a silver spray without any preparation, and the silver makes a dramatic effect in any finished group.

G

The Rolled Paper figures can be made to sit as well as stand. Thrones and chairs for kings or queens can be made from matchboxes or from salvaged cartons. The shape of these can be related to contemporary examples of furniture which you will find illustrated in the reference works. You can add various decorations to any furniture you want to make, using cut sections of balsa wood or cardboard. If these are stuck on in a patterned arrangement before you paint they will add an enriched quality to the final effect.

Rolled Paper Figures —Mounted

The flexibility of the Rolled Paper figure makes it very suitable for use in modelling mounted figures. It will be clear to you, if you have made one of the figures, that it can be placed astride a horse, and can be used as a Knight or Cavalry figure. The problem of the horse is not difficult.

When you were very young you were probably treated at some time to a 'horse' ride on an adult's back. The adult, in an attempt to amuse you, might have gone down on all fours and pretended to be a horse. If you can remember an incident like this, you will see that it is not so far from the figure made with newspaper rolls to a form which can represent a horse.

In the diagram illustrated (Fig. 49) you can see how variations in the Rolled Paper figure will make a basic form for a horse.

As with the human figure, the leg and the arm sections can be made separately. Instead of feet and hands you will need a simple hoof shape at the ends of both sections.

When you fix the sections together the front legs can remain stiff. The body can be fixed in a horizontal position, and the rear legs can be positioned and bent to suggest the stance of a horse.

Instead of a head on this model you will need a neck, fairly long and sloping like a horse's, and a head sloping in the right direction.

If you have a long enough wire when you join the body it can extend from the tail round the legs and through the body, and up to the nose.

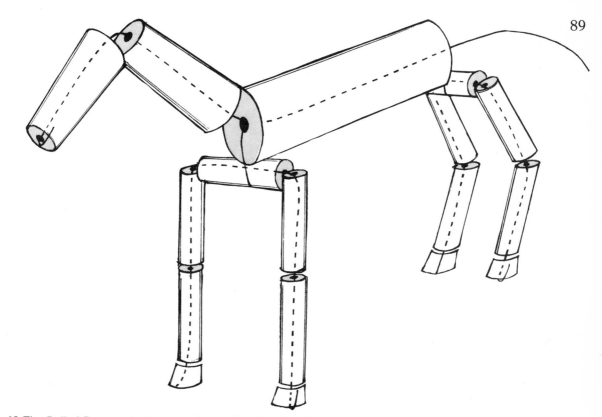

Fig. 49 The Rolled Paper technique may be used to develop the basic shape of a horse for mounted figures.

After you have made the basic shape you will need to use gummed tape at the joints to stop the legs buckling or splaying open where you do not want them to.

A simple head can be modelled with paste-soaked newspaper, but this does not have to be a work of fine sculpture. In many historical models much of the horse's head will be covered by harness or by protective armour.

The mounted knights (Fig. 50) are made as Rolled Paper figures and are seated on horses made by the same technique.

The armour they are wearing is a much simplified version of the type generally worn by mounted figures of the period. This can be dramatic if the modelling is done with a silver-faced cardboard. You might have to hunt around to find a retailer who stocks such a card, but if you can find it it should not be excessively expensive to buy.

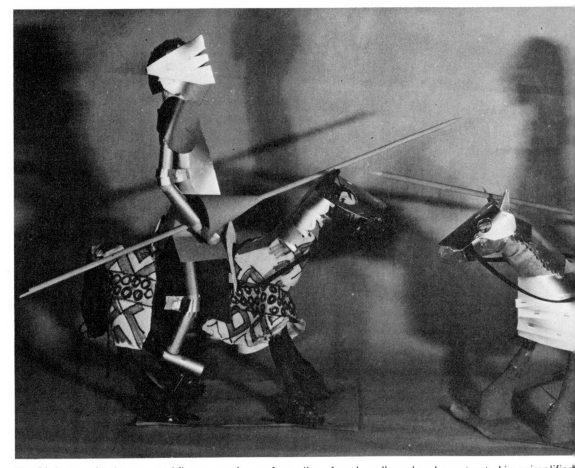

Fig. 50 Armour for the mounted figures can be cut from silver-faced cardboard and constructed in a simplified way slotted, or turned and fixed at the back.

A single sheet of cardboard will go a long way if you plan your work carefully. Before cutting it you should make patterns in wrapping paper, and when you are going to cut the final model you should arrange the patterns so that you get a minimum amount of wasted card. It is easy to cut indiscriminately when you know the shape you want, but a little careful planning will save money.

For an armoured figure it is not necessary to try imitating the suit of armour in exact detail. You should find a reference source with clear illustrations and you should pick out some of the simpler main features for your model.

The helmet will probably be quite difficult. It is not possible to make a dished shape from the flat card,

so you should try to find a way of building it from strips or separate sections.

The helmet can be started with an ordinary headband, which will fit the model's head, and over which you can fit strips of cardboard (Fig. 51). The drawing is simplified to show the possible construction. When this method is used for an actual model the strips can be placed closer together so that the end effect will be more solid than in the diagram.

The 'visor and beaver', which protect the front of the face, can be cut from folded cardboard so that they are sharp at the front (Fig. 52). These can be fixed with paper fasteners at the sides of the helmet *aa*, so that they can be raised and lowered like a real helmet.

An alternative method of constructing the helmet is illustrated (Fig. 53), in which—again starting with a headband—the strips are placed from front to back, and from side to side. They can be stapled on the headband and at the point of overlap at the top.

For the rest of the armour a simple 'breast' can be cut on the fold (Fig. 54). It can incorporate flaps for bending over the shoulders *a*, and can be cut large enough to allow for an overlapping fixture at the back *b*.

Fig. 51 The form of the helmet can be developed on a headband.

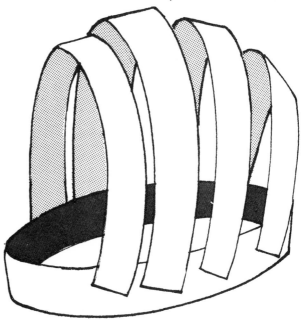

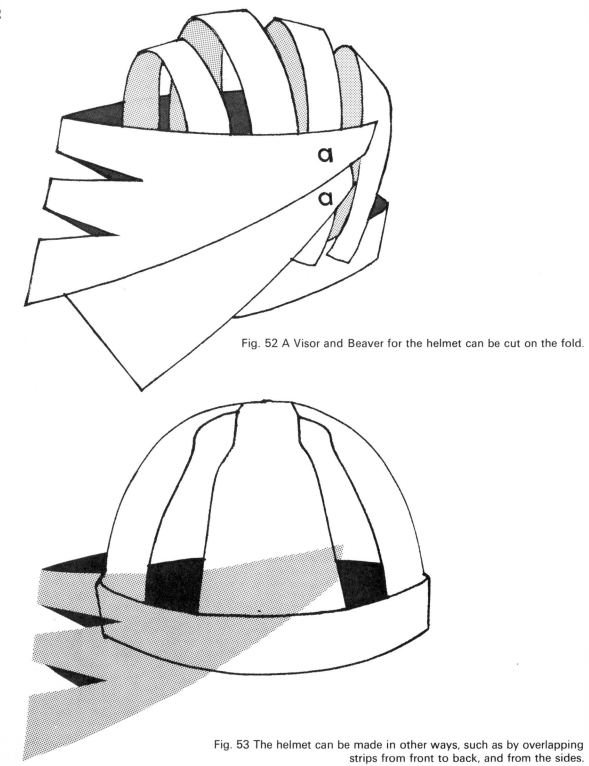

Fig. 52 A Visor and Beaver for the helmet can be cut on the fold.

Fig. 53 The helmet can be made in other ways, such as by overlapping strips from front to back, and from the sides.

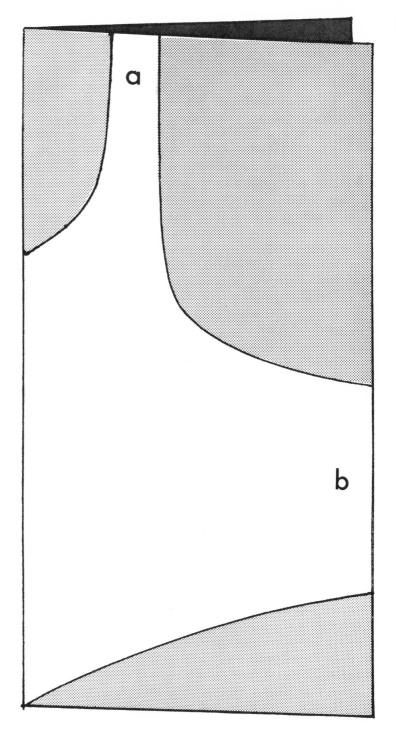

Fig. 54 Body armour can be developed in simple shapes.
The Breast can be cut on the fold, with flaps for fixing.

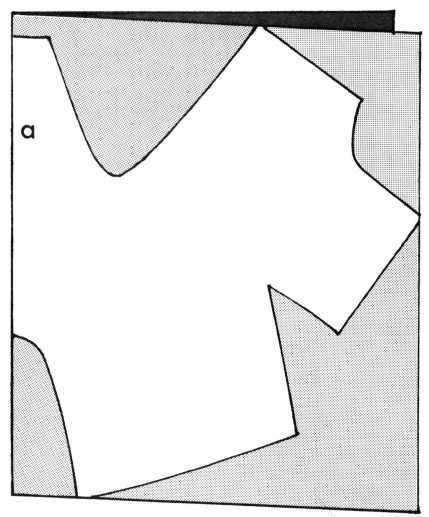

Fig. 55 A Tasset or skirt can be cut on the fold with an extension for tucking under the breast.

A 'tasset' or skirt can also be cut on the fold (Fig. 55), with a front section *a* which can be tucked up under the breast. The skirt must be open, with a cut-away portion at the front, so that the armoured figure can be seated astride the horse. The tasset can also overlap and be fixed at the back.

In the completed figure (Fig. 56) final suggestions of detail can include simple 'gauntlets', simple elbow pieces, 'couters'; and knee pieces, 'poleyns'. The rest of the figure need not be dressed. It can be sprayed silver as in the illustration (Fig. 50).

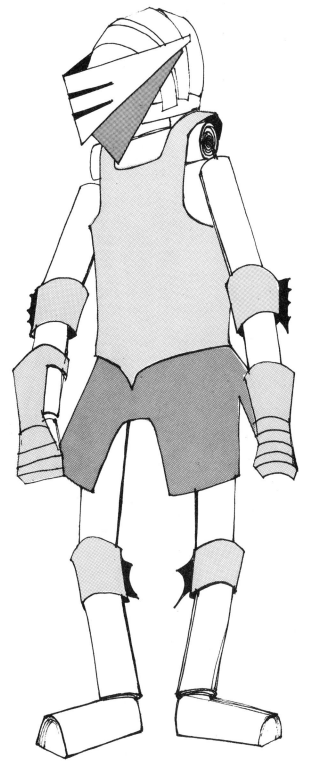

Fig. 56 Some parts of the Rolled Paper figure can be dressed in armour.
The rest can be painted silver.

The words used to describe pieces of this armour, such as couters, poleyn and tasset, are probably new words to you. They are no longer in common usage in our language because we no longer need them, unless we are specialists concerned with historical research. If you are modelling a historical figure, and if you are doing the appropriate research, the words will mean something to you because you will be involved with the things they describe. You will find that words like this can soon become a part of your own vocabulary.

Simple armour for the horses can be made in the same way as that for the figures. A 'peytral' and 'crupper', the armour protections for the front and back of the horse's body, can be made from strips of cardboard stapled together. The armourers would have made them originally by riveting strips of metal together so that the shapes could be formed to fit the horse's body. This is an interesting link with your own work, in which you also will be taking a material and putting it together in a similar way.

As an alternative to the body armour you may cover part of the horse with a cloth caparison, which can be decorated in colour. The caparison was sometimes simply decorated, and at others was extremely ornate. You can investigate this in your research, and can investigate methods of painting the cloth or of using an appliquéd or even embroidered decoration.

For neck and head protection of the horses the armourers evolved a metal collar and a mask with shielded holes for the eyes. You will find no problem in constructing either of these if you use sections or strips of card stapled together to follow or fit the shape.

It might happen, if you have worked on this section of the book, that you will find yourself developing an interest in armour of various periods. This may be caused partly because there is a real link between making armour in cardboard for a model and making the real thing in metal.

If you are working in cardboard you have to cut appropriate shapes, and to establish form by fixing them together. Small staples are a suitable substitute for the armourer's metal stitch or rivet, and to make shapes for a knight or his horse you will have to construct in sections as the armourer did, attaching one suitably-shaped piece to another.

The study of armour can become fascinating if you work in this way. If you become interested you might build yourself a collection of armoured figures from different periods of history.

If you find yourself interested but unable to get a suitable silver-faced board, you can use any plain card sprayed with silver. You can also use card covered with kitchen foil. For the best effect with this method the foil, which can be glued to the base with a thin adhesive, should be stuck in small sections at a time, otherwise it is difficult to eliminate crinkling.

There were, of course, many different types of armour used at different periods of history. Reference sources, many of them published by museums, will describe with illustrations almost any period in which you are interested, and after making preliminary researches you can create the models. The Rolled Paper figures and horses can be developed to illustrate any style or period of historical costume.

Puppet People

If you take a box, an empty package of some sort—preferably with a plain undecorated surface on one side—and if you open an end so that you can slip your hand into it, you do not alter it. It remains a box. You can move your hand about with the box on it, and you can talk out loud, but there is nothing special about the box. It is just an empty pack.

If, however, you draw or paint two eyes on the plain surface, and a simple triangular nose, you will change the box and will immediately give it an identity. If you now put the box on your hand and speak out loud, it may appear as though you are intending to speak through the identity of the character you have created.

The empty pack is no longer what it was because you have made it into a very simple puppet. This is not likely to be a very good puppet, but it might be the first step towards some deliberate work in creating characters—even towards having a puppet theatre of your own.

You might have found in earlier exercises, when you made figures, that you were at times inclined to speak to them, or even for them. This is sometimes inevitable when you are making figures and are trying to give them an identity.

There are, of course, many ways of making puppets. The craft of puppet theatre in various forms has a long history and extends widely throughout the world. There are many sources you can go to if you want to develop a skill in traditional methods of puppetry. These are available as specialist books on the subject. But some of the traditional methods are highly involved and skilled, and some of the methods used take a long time before you can see the results or use the puppet figures.

There are, however, some simpler ways which can be evolved with inexpensive materials like paper and cardboard. Some of these are natural developments from the work with figures which you might already have attempted.

The salvaged box or container which can be made into a face is one of the simplest puppets. There are many sorts of hollow shape which can be used, from the inner core of tissue rolls to any other sort of household package which can be placed over the fingers and which has a suitable surface for painting or decorating.

The cones (Fig. 57), salvaged from a textile mill, illustrate some of the various methods which can be used to create a puppet face. These cones are in pressed board and will take most adhesives and paints, both of which can be sometimes troublesome when plastic cartons are used.

A combination of painted features and added materials will make the salvaged pack into a puppet head. Eyes must usually be painted as white shapes with dark pupils, otherwise the puppet will sometimes appear to be blind; but painting generally need only be used to support added features, which can be made from a variety of materials. Most of these also can be salvaged from throw-away sources.

The use of straw or wool for hair will obviously make a desirable contrast to the solid shape, and will give added form to the head. Paper hair is a simple

Fig. 57 A variety of salvaged shapes and containers can be used as the basis for a puppet head.

possibility. It can be cut and stuck in sections, and the hair can be curled in the way described for the single-fold Santa Claus, shown in Fig. 32. String and rope can be frayed to make effective hair and whiskers, and can be used as alternatives to cotton waste, shredded paper or other packing materials.

It is sometimes effective to arrange and stick hair to a puppet head methodically, working to a system. If you consider the way the hair grows on your own head you might realize that, if you were covering the head yourself, you would start with the hair at the lower back of your neck and would work gradually upwards to the crown.

For features you can use almost any material which can be shaped. A material which cuts as easily as cork has obviously some potential, especially the round cross-section which can be used for protruding eyes.

Paper and card noses and other features can be used as in previous exercises. This is a quick method of establishing a puppet face, and it is effective because the simple exaggerated style is very theatrical.

There are now various forms of plastic available which can be used for puppet heads. You will have seen these used in component packaging or in the home as insulating tiles. They cut easily and can be stuck with suitable adhesives, which makes them very suitable for shape and feature work in puppetry. As in previous exercises it will be necessary, if you are going to use these materials, to find the right adhesive which will bond the plastics to the background.

The question of identity for a puppet is one which must be left to the puppet maker. It is the materials he chooses and the way in which he puts them together which will determine the final result. There are as many possibilities in the constructed puppet as there are possibilities in drawn faces. The cone (Fig. 57) is the same in each example, but different treatments with a variety of materials have produced different effects. It is a good field for experiment and fun.

While many puppet shapes and identities are possible with salvaged materials, there may still be a point where—for a play or merely for fun—you might prefer to make an actual puppet.

In the past, one of the traditional ways of doing this was to start with a core of modelling material, clay or Plasticine, and after shaping the head in it, to cover it with layers of pasted paper which would eventually dry to a workable hardness. This would allow the later removal of the inner core.

This is a well-established method for making light and very durable puppet heads, but it has the disadvantage of taking a long time. There are simpler and quicker ways.

It is possible to make an adequate Glove Puppet in
less than an hour, and—using paper—at almost no
cost.

Stage 1
You should begin with a rectangle of fairly stiff paper
about the size of this page. If you are starting with
a standard (Imperial) size sheet, you can use an eighth
of the sheet.

This piece of paper should be rolled into a cylinder,
as tall as the longer dimension. It should be possible
to slide the cylinder over the middle and forefinger
of your hand.

It is important to make the cylinder of a size which
will go over your fingers easily. This is because you
will need to slip the puppet on and off without having
to force your fingers into it. You must not, however,
make the cylinder too loose, otherwise it will flop about
when you want to work with it.

The lower part of this cylinder will form the neck
of your puppet, and should be fixed in the cylindrical
position with a few layers of gummed tape.

Stage 2
Take a double-page sheet of newspaper and fold it
several times—in either direction—to make a strip
which, when it is rolled, will form the puppet head.
The width of this strip will roughly establish the height
of the puppet face.

It should be wound round your first cylinder, leaving
the neck protruding at the base (Fig. 58). You should
wind it firmly, but it should not buckle the original
cylinder. It can be stuck with gummed strip.

At this stage you will have a squat and fairly thick
cylinder of newspaper, with an inner cylindrical
core protruding from the top and bottom.

Stage 3
You can now fold the top section of your original
cylinder down over the rolled newspaper. When you
have folded it firmly it can be stuck with gummed
tape (Fig. 59).

This will establish the front of the puppet head, and
you might find it possible even at this stage to intro-

Fig. 58 A puppet head can be modelled with
a roll of newspaper on a cylinder.

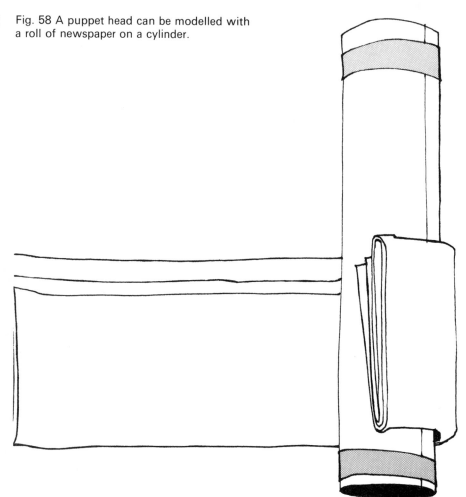

duce a little modelling by shaping a chin as you fold
the cylinder down, although this is not essential.

After this stage you should be able to hold the basic
head on your fingers. You should be able to see its
potential.

Stage 4
You should prepare for this stage by putting down
newspapers as a protection on your working surface.
It is a slightly messy stage.

You will need some paper-hanger's paste—the old-
fashioned type or the more modern plastic version
can both be used. The advantage of the second type
is that it will last longer after mixing without going
bad. You will also need some torn pieces of newspaper,

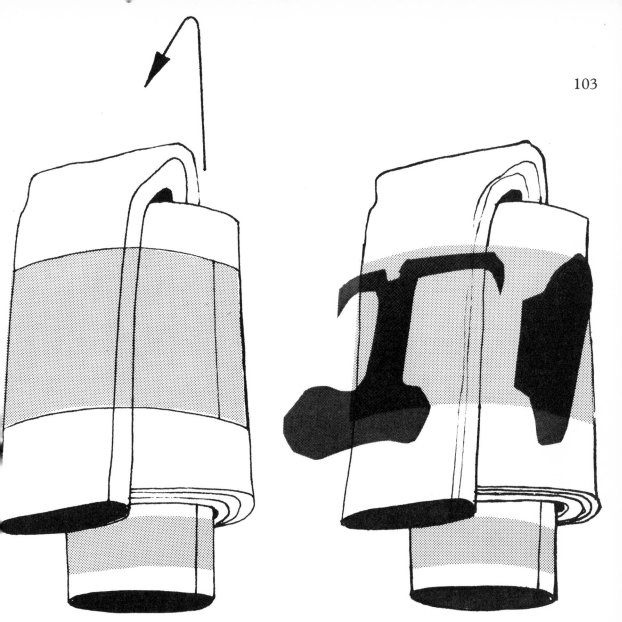

ig. 59 The top of the inner cylinder must be
ent over and secured with gummed strip.

Fig. 60 Features can be added to the head
with papier-mâché.

about half the size of this page; and some pieces of
tissue paper torn slightly smaller.

If you impregnate the newspaper pieces with paste
you will make a type of papier-mâché, which can be
modelled as features on the front of the puppet head
(Fig. 60). When you are making the papier-mâché
you can dip the newspaper into the paste, or paste it
liberally with a brush, but before you model—when
the paper is thoroughly impregnated—you should
squeeze out as much excess paste as possible.

H

As you apply the features you can build them up and develop a character and style. They can be made permanent with overpasted layers of tissue paper, which can be modelled into the features. You will find it adequate to put on two or three layers of tissue paper.

If you can buy a pink tissue paper it will make a useful finishing effect, but any sort of tissue can be used, even the salvaged wrappings from fruit or other bought articles.

During this stage you can model in as much detail as you please, although you should again remember that you are working close to the head and that it will really be viewed from a distance. The simple exaggerated effect, which you should already be familiar with, will work better than any amount of fussy detail.

When you are satisfied with the features of your puppet it must be left to dry. You will see at this stage why it was necessary to squeeze out the excess paste as you were working.

The drying process can be speeded up if you can leave the head overnight on a radiator, or near some other source of heat, although obviously a protective paper should be placed between the wet head and any clean surface.

When the head is finally dry you should find it light enough to be used comfortably, and hard enough to be durable.

Stage 5

After drying, the head can be painted and trimmed with hair or other features. If you are using string or rope as hair you can stiffen it with cold water size so that it will remain in any shape you want.

The glove for the puppet (Fig. 61) can be made as a simple shape to fit the hand. It can be made in the shape illustrated, but cut double and sewn at the sides.

The glove should have a slit at the top, where it can be tacked to the neck with simple stitches. It can also be fixed with a rubber band or with a suitable adhesive. Since it will be partly seen during any performance the glove can have its own simple decorative treatment.

Fig. 61 Glove puppets can be made very quickly, using newspaper rolled round a cylinder.

This method of making a puppet can be used for any sort of character. The modelling in stage four is what will really decide the final result, and you can afford to be quite dramatic and adventurous at this stage. There is no reason to be tentative or hesitant. You are using inexpensive materials, and if you go wrong you can always start again.

If you want the puppet to have a particular feature, a large nose for example, you should make the feature extra large—and then you should add a little bit more. It will almost certainly convey the right quality in the final puppet, and it is very unlikely that you will ever make a feature too exaggerated for a puppet theatre.

A puppet stage for this sort of glove puppet can be made in a number of ways. A simple one, without any background, can be established immediately by turning a table on its side so that the puppet operators can work from behind it.

It is sometimes possible now to find large packing cases in which refrigerators and other large pieces of equipment are delivered to retailers. By asking around you might find one of these which can be converted into a simple stage by removing a front opening for the play, and part of the back for the operators' entrance.

If you are interested in puppetry you will find a way of making a stage, and ways of painting and hanging drops and scenery.

It is possible, of course, to make puppets without giving performances with them. They can be made for pleasure, or as part of a collection, or they can be given away as presents. You would not find it strange to buy a puppet at a toyshop and give it as a present to someone.

But puppetry really is a joint activity in which a number of people collaborate in making the performance. It is a very suitable activity for school use, as many of you will already know, because you can bring to life so many things with the puppet figures.

If you do not have any opportunity for puppet work in school you might make one or two of these simple glove puppets, and might try to persuade your teacher to let a group of you make some more.   107

If a number of you work together you will find that the activity can benefit you all in many ways. When there are a number of you involved you will have more sources to tap for wools and other trimmings, and you will have a more lively work potential when you pool your ideas.

A group of you working together might soon reach the standard where your work will justify public performance. You can then get more people involved, with background music or with sound effects, perhaps using a tape recorder. The use of lighting and the dramatic effects of colour change are also possibilities which can be explored when there is a large enough group involved.

All of these can be developed in a puppet show in which the characters are made from newspaper.

Paper Puppets   Although the glove puppets made from newspaper can be completed quickly, there are even quicker ways of making a workable hand puppet. There are also simpler and less messy ways, which might be an advantage if, for example, you are in hospital or confined to bed in your own room.

If you are unable for some reason to use the pasted newspaper method, or if you want a puppet which can be used immediately without having to wait some hours for it to dry, you can construct the head on a simple basic form in paper.

This can be cut on the fold so that it will be symmetrical when it is opened out. It can include flaps at the side to make a fixture possible at the back of the operator's hand. A suitable basic shape is illustrated in the diagram (Fig. 62).

The actual shape may be varied to suit the character you want to portray. It can be long and thin, or it can be rounded in shape like the illustration. It can have a tall forehead or a double chin, or any other feature you like. But first you should make the basic shape similar to the one shown. This can be cut from thick paper or from thin cardboard. You will remember that the centre fold will introduce a certain amount of strength to the material.

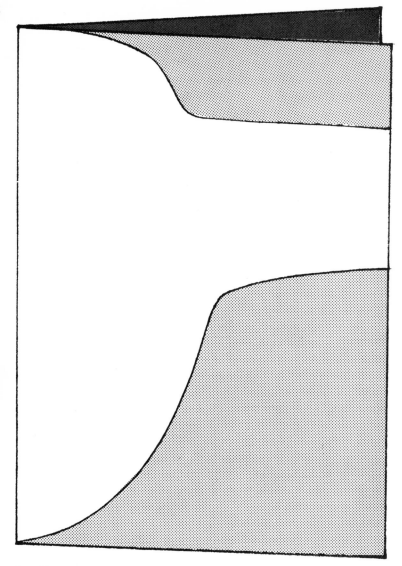

Fig. 62 The basic shape for a Paper Puppet can be cut on the fold with flaps for fixing included.

The flaps which are included at the side of the shape can make a simple locking fixture for the back of the hand, eliminating the need for any pasting. They should be cut with slots on one side at the top (Fig. 63) *a*, and on the other side at the bottom *b*.

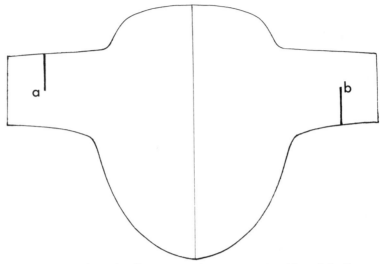

Fig. 63 Slots for a dry fixture must be on opposite sides of the flaps.

This is a simple technique which you might need to practise. The distance from the slot to the edge of the flap should be the same on both sides. If they are cut in the right position, the flaps can be taken round to the back of the shape, and can be slotted together (Fig. 64). When you make this fixture you should try to get the ends of both flaps on the inside of the form. It is possible. When you have made the fixture the end part of the flap on both sides should not be visible.

After locking the flaps together you will have a band at the back of the face shape which will allow you to slip it over three fingers of one of your hands, leaving the thumb and small finger free. These can serve as simple arms (Fig. 65).

This is now another example of a basic shape on which you can work in any way you like. Additions to the shape can be cut from different coloured papers, and if these are cut with flaps included you will be able to complete the figures without any sticking problems. The flaps can be inserted through slots cut in the main shape, and can be folded down to make the fixture permanent. To make the fixtures even more permanent the flaps can be stuck down at the back with transparent sticky tape.

Features in this type of paper puppet must be kept

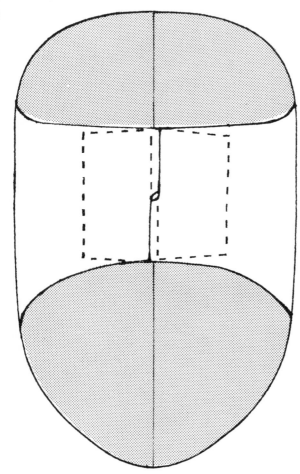

Fig. 64 When the slots are put together as a fixture the ends of the flaps should be on the inside.

as simple as possible. It will also help to make them as large as possible.

A simple glove for the puppet can be cut similar to the shape illustrated (Fig. 66). This should be narrow at the waist so that your thumb and small finger can be seen at the sides. It can be cut incorporating its own locking device as in the flaps at the back of the head.

In Fig. 66 it might appear that the slots at *a* and *b* are on the same side, but this is in fact not so. If you could flatten the curve of the neck you would find that one slot would be at the top, and the other at the bottom of the flaps.

Fig. 65 Paper Puppets can be worked with the operator's thumb and little finger as the arms.

To cut an original pattern for this shape you can use the method described in a previous exercise. You can make a pattern to fit your own hand, making the final version neat and symmetrical by folding it vertically through the middle. You could use this afterwards as a flat pattern, since the glove part of the paper puppet does not really benefit from a fold through the centre.

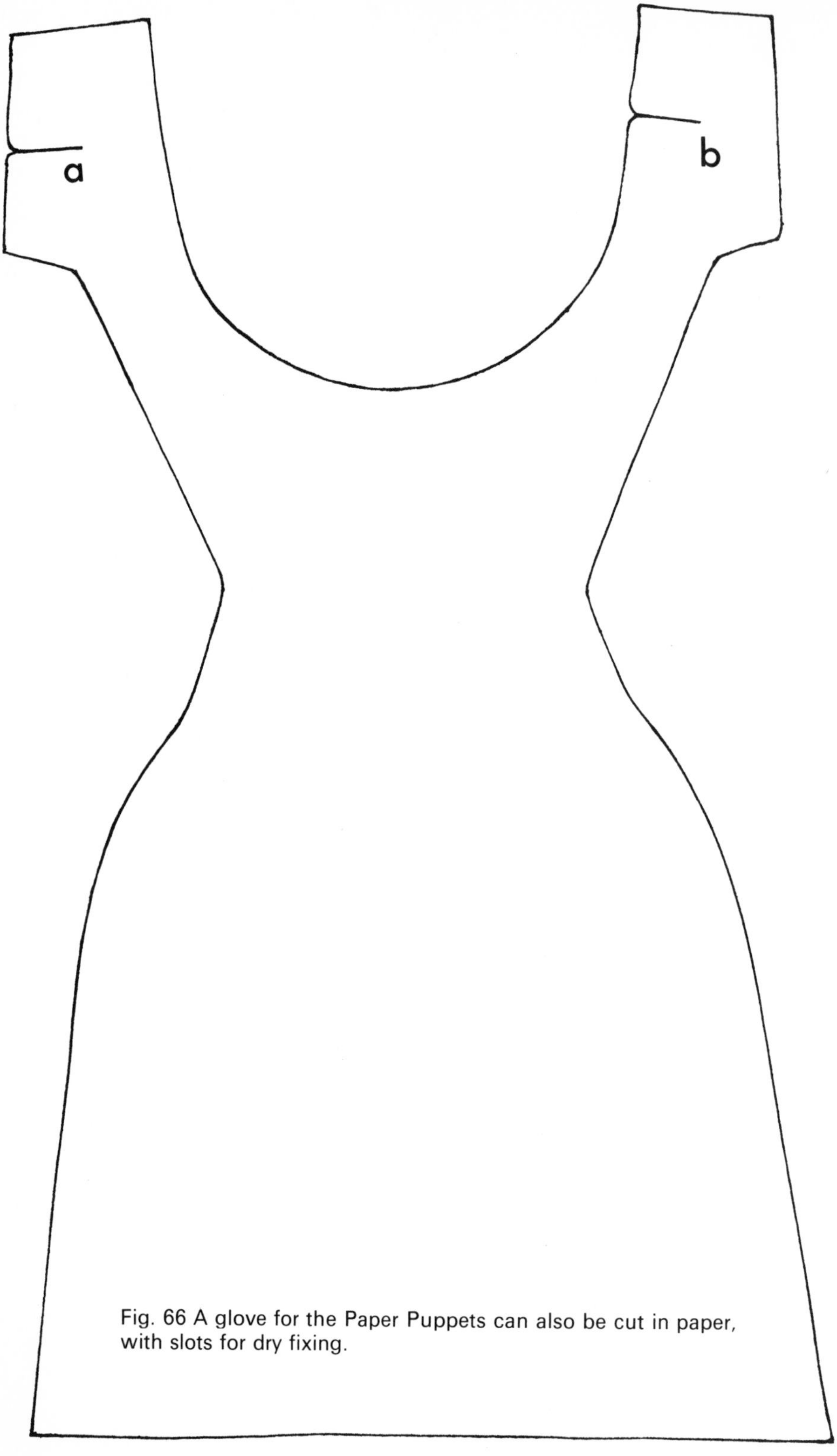

a

b

Fig. 66 A glove for the Paper Puppets can also be cut in paper, with slots for dry fixing.

Punch and Judy You will have seen that the Paper Puppets can be exploited to make many different types of character. There is no reason why they should be any less effective than more complex figures.

The Punch and Judy puppets (Fig. 67) have a clearly established identity, although they are made in this method.

The original shape for the Punch face has been cut long and thin. It is developed with a nose and brow shape cut on the fold and including flaps for the fixture. This is illustrated in the diagram (Fig. 68).

The tall hat can be cut separately, and can include flaps for a self-locking fixture at the back (Fig. 69).

Fig. 67 The Paper Puppet can be given as much identity as any other form of puppet.

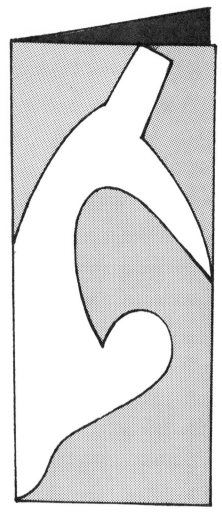

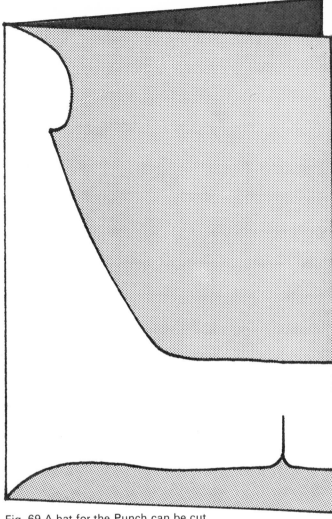

Fig. 68 A nose for the Punch figure can be cut on the fold.

Fig. 69 A hat for the Punch can be cut with flaps for fixing at the back.

The figure is, of course, much assisted by the way it is decorated. Any work on the features, which can be done with felt-tipped pens or with oil crayons, should be gay and decorative rather than realistic.

The Judy figure can incorporate a cap in the basic shape (Fig. 70). This is included at the top of the head, where the curved cut at *a* will allow for a band of hair to be inserted (Fig. 71).

If you cut and use a hair shape in which the hair is long enough, it can be curled to disappear effectively behind the head as in the illustration (Fig. 67).

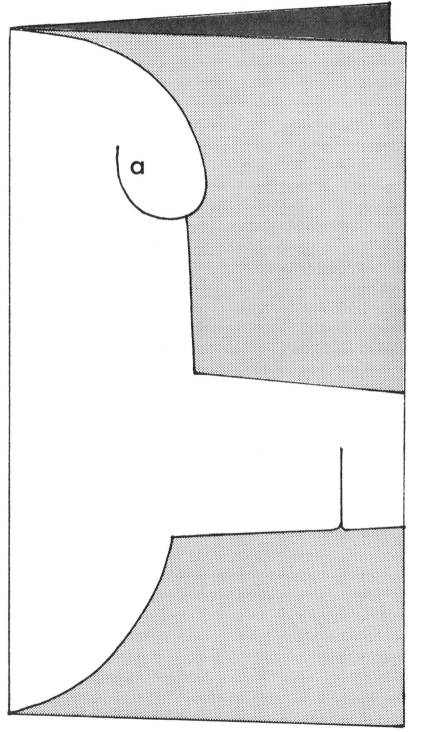

Fig. 70 Variations, like this one for the Judy figure, can be made in the head shape of the Paper Puppets.

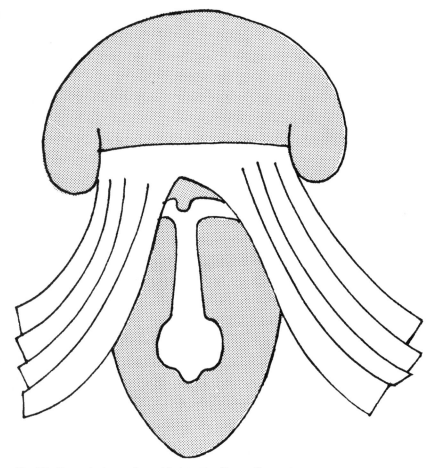

Fig. 71 Paper hair can be added to the Paper Puppet.

Any painted or added treatment to this figure should also be gay and decorative rather than realistic. You might also try to make simple visual effects in the paper gloves by contrasting, for example, curves and stripes—or dark and lighter colours.

These paper puppets are, of course, very much less durable than other types of puppet, but they can be used over and over again if they are made from adequately strong material, and if they are manipulated carefully.

When they are not in use they should be stored in cardboard boxes, and not left lying around where they can easily be crushed. They can also be pinned to the wall, where they will be out of the way.

If you are unfortunate enough to be confined to bed, or if you have a sick friend, you might try some of the Paper Puppets. They are not difficult to make, and they might help to make a convalescence or a stay in hospital a little less tiresome than it would otherwise be—for the patients, and perhaps even for those who are nursing them.

Finger Faces

If you have made Paper Puppets and used them on your hands you will perhaps have amused yourself with some made-up dialogue. There is an even smaller puppet which you can make so that, even if you are lying in bed, you can operate a number of them at the same time.

For the Finger Faces you will again need to start with a basic shape on which you can build the character.

To begin with you will need a cylinder of paper which will fit over your finger. You should make it in fairly stiff paper, using a small stapler to make the fixtures.

A second piece of paper, cut with a hand at each end, and slightly curled, can be fixed to the back of the cylinder to make the basic shape (Fig. 72). This shape must be made so that it can be slipped on and off the finger.

It can be developed with added features cut from a variety of different coloured and patterned papers. These can be fixed with flaps and slots, or they can be stapled if you have one of the very small pocket type staplers.

It is unlikely that you would want one of these figures on all your fingers as in the illustration (Fig. 73). But with one or two on each hand you can make small and rather personal plays for your own amusement.

Working on this scale is of course different from the sort of work you will have done in many of the previous exercises, and must inevitably require more care both in cutting and fixing. There will be some people who might prefer the more intricate processes involved in working at this scale, and others who will

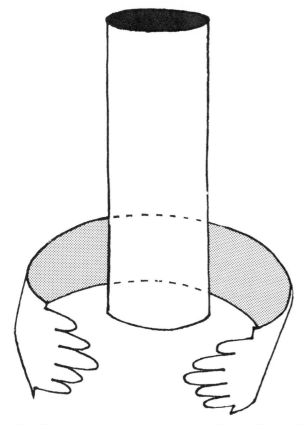

Fig. 72 A basic shape can be made up for the Finger Puppet.

find themselves unable to cope, whose fingers will not respond to the involved requirements of the modelling. It will depend entirely on the person, and is a matter of temperament and aptitude.

There is, however, nothing limiting about the Finger Figures. There are as many simple variations possible when you work this size as there are in any other form of puppetry, both in patterned effect and in feature and characterization (Fig. 74). The figures will obviously never be realistic, but this is good for puppetry. They are not intended to be real figures.

If you are working in bed or in a limited space the Finger Figures might be a good opportunity for occupying yourself creatively when you are tired of reading or listening to the radio. You will need no more than a few pieces of coloured paper, a small pair of scissors and the smallest sort of stapler. The slots for the flaps can be cut with the tips of the scissors

Fig. 73 Finger Puppets might appeal to people who like working on a small size, or to patients in hospital who have limited space and little material.

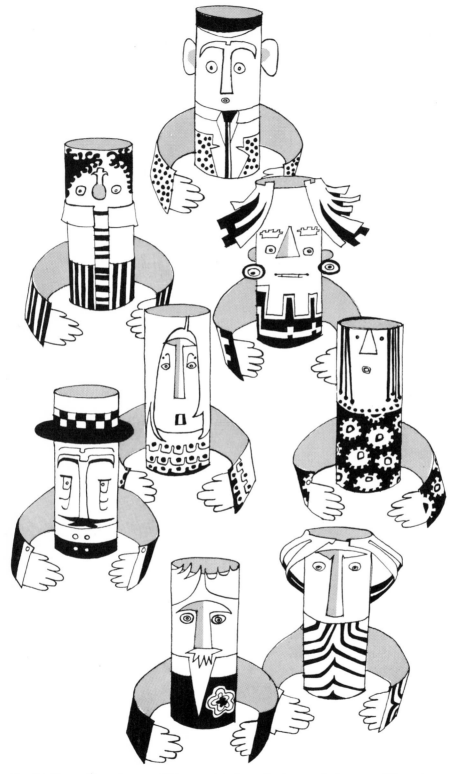

Fig. 74 Finger Puppets can still be used to investigate people in many different ways.

if you pinch the paper carefully at the points where you want them in the basic forms. You must cut with care so that you do not crush the form, but this is something which you can master quickly if you understand what you are doing. It is a question of care and a little practice.

It could be interesting, if you are in hospital, to occupy yourself making Finger Figures of your relatives. You could then give them to them when they visited you. This would vary the usual hospital procedure in which the visitor is the one who does the giving, and would tell your visitors that you also think of them when they are not there.

Moving Figures   If you have made and operated any of the puppets you have actually been involved with figures which move. Even the small Finger Figures have a certain movement potential. You can make them bend and you can turn them.

The human figure is a thing which moves all the time, and if we are making figures—even as small models—and giving them identities, we can extend the process wherever we can introduce movement.

There are various different ways in which model figures can be constructed to incorporate movement. With hand and finger puppets the movement is actually that of the operator, but there are figures which can be made with their own moving parts and which only partly depend on an operator.

Newspaper Marionettes   When you were making the Rolled Paper Figures (Fig. 46, page 82), you wound newspaper rolls on a wire armature so that the figure could be made to assume a variety of positions.

An identical figure made on a string armature will serve as the basic form for a marionette which can be manually controlled, and which can be made to perform a range of different movements.

The marionette figure can be made in exactly the same way as the standing figure. You should start

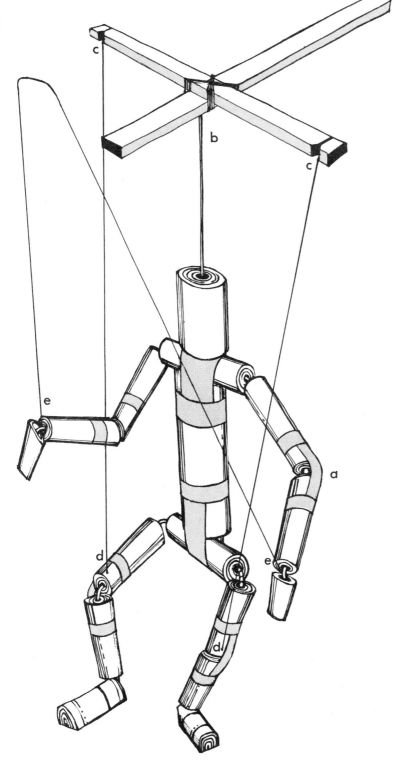

Fig. 75 The Rolled Paper figures developed on a flexible armature can be used as marionettes.

with the separate section for the hands and arms, but this time you must wind your rolls round a reasonably strong—but not over-thick—string. The sort used for tying small parcels will do.

You must then make the feet and leg section, which can be attached to the body and then to the shoulders and head. The backbone or attachment must be made also with string, which should not be tied off at the head like the wire, but which should extend above the head so that the marionette can be fixed to its control.

At this stage the figure will be hopelessly floppy, with the various parts able to move freely in all directions. This is, of course, not like a human body—try turning your own arm round and round at the elbow—and you must impose some limit on the movement potential.

In the diagram (Fig. 75) various points are suggested for imposed control.

The body should be fixed at the shoulders and at the hips, so that neither the arm nor the leg sections can revolve independently. This fixture can be made with gummed strip.

At the elbows there should be only limited movement A simple hinge can be evolved by fixing a strip of tape across the opening of the joint, (Fig. 75a).

To make this joint, you should cut a small strip of tape—bandage or cloth can be used if tape is not available—and two pieces of gummed strip. The top of the tape can be fixed with the gummed strip to the upper arm. It can then be fixed to the upper end of the forearm, allowing enough movement at the joint for an up and down gesture, like a normal arm, but preventing complete rotation.

A similar hinge can also be made at the other elbow, and at both knee joints.

For an even more refined control the hinge can also be introduced at both hips, but this is not essential.

The effect of these hinges will be to limit the movement of the limbs, but the hinge must in no case be made too tightly to inhibit an easy raising and lowering of the arm or leg.

You can experiment with your figure at this stage. Holding the figure upright with the feet on a flat surface, you should place a finger under the thigh and raise it from the vertical to horizontal position. The leg must bend of its own accord at the knee.

When you take your finger away, the leg should drop freely to its original position, and should not remain stiff or bent.

In the same way it should be possible to raise the arm from its position at the side of the body, and to drop it freely back again.

It may be necessary at this stage to secure the feet to the ankles, if your original tying off is too loose. When you raise the leg the foot should remain in its horizontal position. If it tends to drop it can be fixed more securely with gummed tape.

When you have reached this stage you can string the marionette to its control.

For a hand control you will need a simple wooden cross. This can be of very thin section wood, which can be lashed with thread at the crossing point, where it will probably be too thin for any sort of nailed joint.

The central string of the figure can be tied to the control at the point of intersection b. The height of this fixture will be determined by the size of the operator, or the distance between the puppet stage and the operators' platform (Fig. 76).

When you make the wooden control you should cut a notch at the two ends of the cross piece c, so that the strings which will be attached can be tied without any danger of their slipping off.

You can now fix a separate thread to each knee d. For stringing and operating the puppet a cotton thread is better than nylon, which tends to knot easily where you do not want it to. The thread can be pierced through the knees, using a strong needle, and tied off at the back. Or it can be fixed in place with gummed strip.

After fixing the threads at the knees you will need someone to help you. You should get them to hold the figure upright, with one hand on the control and with the other hand holding the feet together so that the marionette is stretched to the full length of the main string b.

With your helper keeping the figure taut you can now tie the leg threads to the control on each side c.

The reason why the figure should be kept taut

Fig. 76 The Rolled Paper marionette, operated with a simple
control, can be made to move
through a variety of positions
suitable for public performance.

Fig. 77 A cheap but effective marionette can be made from rolled newspaper and scraps of cloth

Fig. 78 The marionette can be adequately large and can be strung to be operated from a comfortable height.

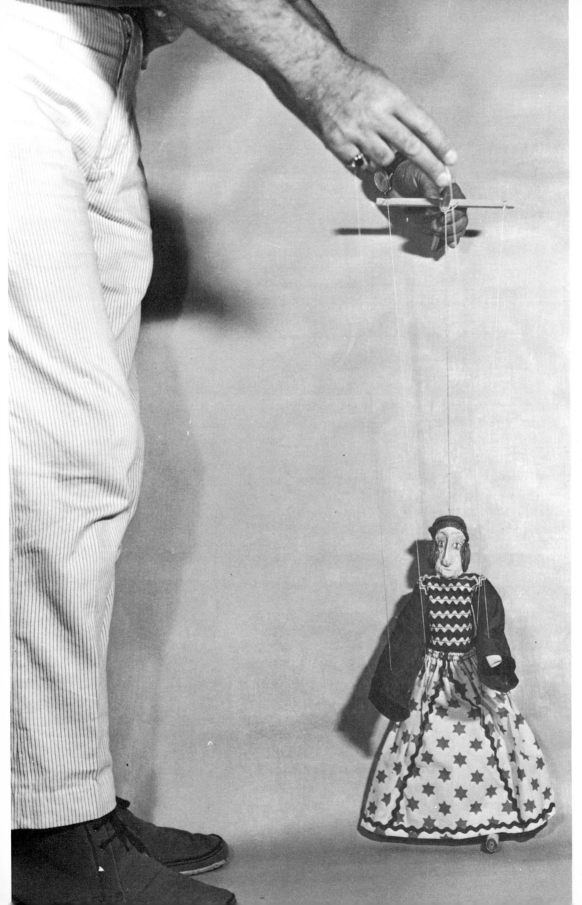

during this part of the stringing operation, is because you must have both of these threads of equal length, and the bar should be horizontal when the marionette is in a normal standing position.

By moving the horizontal bar up and down at the sides—a movement which should be possible merely by rotating the wrist slightly—the legs of the figure should lift and lower in turn. If at the same time the controller's hand moves in a direction taking the marionette forward, the figure will appear to be walking.

This method of walking a marionette has to be practised like any other skill, but it can be quickly mastered if the stringing is correct.

Another thread can now be tied in a continuous loop from one wrist of the marionette to the other e, so that the arms can be manipulated by the operator with his free hand (Fig. 78).

When you have the strings in place you will find that it is possible to make the marionette perform a number of different actions. It can be made to walk forwards or back, to sit or to kneel, and to raise its arms, either together or separately.

For your first exercises in which you will be getting familiar with the control and learning to make the marionette respond, it will be useful to practise with the rolled paper figure before it is dressed (Fig. 76).

When you feel you can operate it with some fluency, this figure can be used as a basic shape for any character developments you like to make.

You can model features on the head with the papier-mâché and overlapping tissue paper method, and you can add hair and simple painted eyes and lips.

You can also dress the marionettes. This can be done before adding the strings. After fixing the thread at the knees it must be threaded in a needle and brought through the front of the skirt or trouser legs.

The dressed figure, with modelled features and hair, will effectively hide the original newspaper construction (Fig. 77), and will make your marionettes very adequate for public performance.

This is a simple and uncostly marionette, but it cannot be made in a few minutes. The craft of string puppets demands from anyone involved in it, patience and a measure of care. If you have these you can develop the skill which will make your marionettes a success.

The instructions which you have just read may seem long and complicated, but if you follow them stage by stage—working as you go along—you will both make and, through seeing the results, you will understand what you are doing. This understanding is an essential part of your work, because there is no real skill without understanding.

When you understand, your skill will improve, your interest will grow and you will find your own ways of improving the processes involved. These are set out and illustrated as points of departure, from which you can make a personal development as a craftsman.

When you can make and operate a marionette you have a whole world of theatre waiting to be investigated. In the home you can have a marionette stage at floor level by stringing a curtain or cloth across the room so that its bottom edge hangs just above the top level of your marionettes when they are standing.

The operators of your play can be hidden behind an upturned table, or behind any board supported on its edge.

If you have room to develop a more permanent theatre there are various books on puppetry which will tell you how to build a simple proscenium, and how to prepare and use scenery.

But you do not need a theatre in order to work with the marionettes. In the home or in the classroom an audience will soon forget the operators as they get involved with the performance of the marionette figures. They will be much more interested in these, and what they have to say, than in the ordinary people operating them.

When you have spent some time making a Paper Marionette, you do not have to wait for an audience. If you have made it yourself you will probably become quite fond of it. You could take it anywhere and would probably want to—even when you do humdrum things like shopping or other errands.

Whatever you do with it, the great thing about a marionette is that it is always a very obedient servant.

When you make a figure with joints, like the Paper Marionette, the figure is articulated and capable of movement because of the joints. The marionette is a three-dimensional figure which requires quite a lot of construction and modelling, but various articulated figures can be made more simply. These can provide lots of opportunities for fun and surprise effects.

In flat articulated figures, which should be cut from cardboard, the articulation is achieved through the use of paper fasteners—the sort with two prongs which can be opened out after piercing the material—or by punching and eyeletting cards together.

An eyelet punch works in two stages. Firstly it punches a hole through the cardboard, and in the second stage it compresses a brass or coloured eyelet through the hole. In some schools this sort of punch will be available, but for all the articulated figures suggested the method with the paper fastener can be used.

When paper fasteners are used the holes should be made large enough to allow a very free movement at any articulated joint. They can be made with a punch or with a sharp point before the fastener is inserted. A bradawl or even a nail can be used if a punch is not available.

For a first exercise in articulated movement with flat figures you can try the two shapes which expand and contract. This early exercise will help you to understand the principle.

The diagram (Fig. 79) illustrates two large shapes joined together by smaller ones.

On the lower shape two extensions are fixed at the sides with paper fasteners *a*. These are joined at their ends to similar shapes fixed at the top shape *b*.

This is a simple method of joining the two shapes which will allow you to open and close the gap between them. It is a way of linking the shapes together permanently. If you make this example you will see that there is in fact much more than a simple up and down movement.

This can be illustrated best by making the shapes into simple figures, and the linking pieces into arms. The acrobats illustrated (Fig. 80) are an example of the way the shapes can be developed.

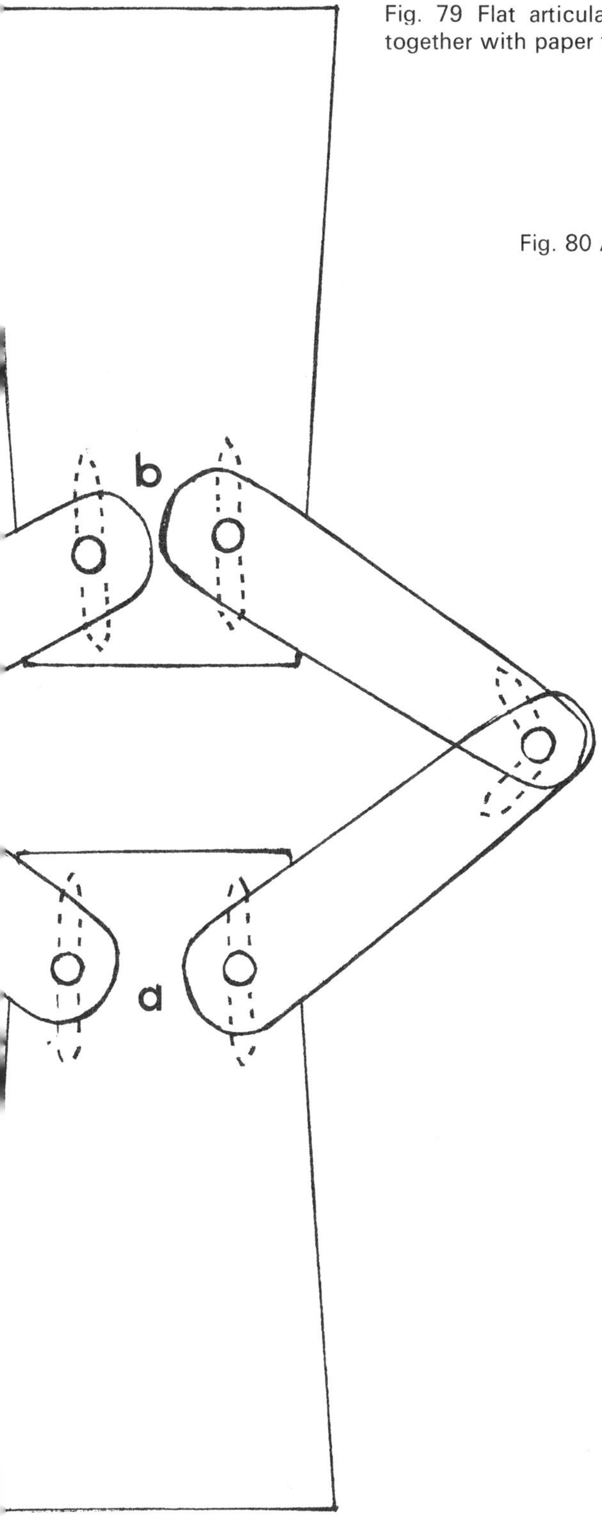

Fig. 79 Flat articulated figures can be developed on shapes fixed together with paper fasteners.

Fig. 80 Articulated figures can make simple amusing toys.

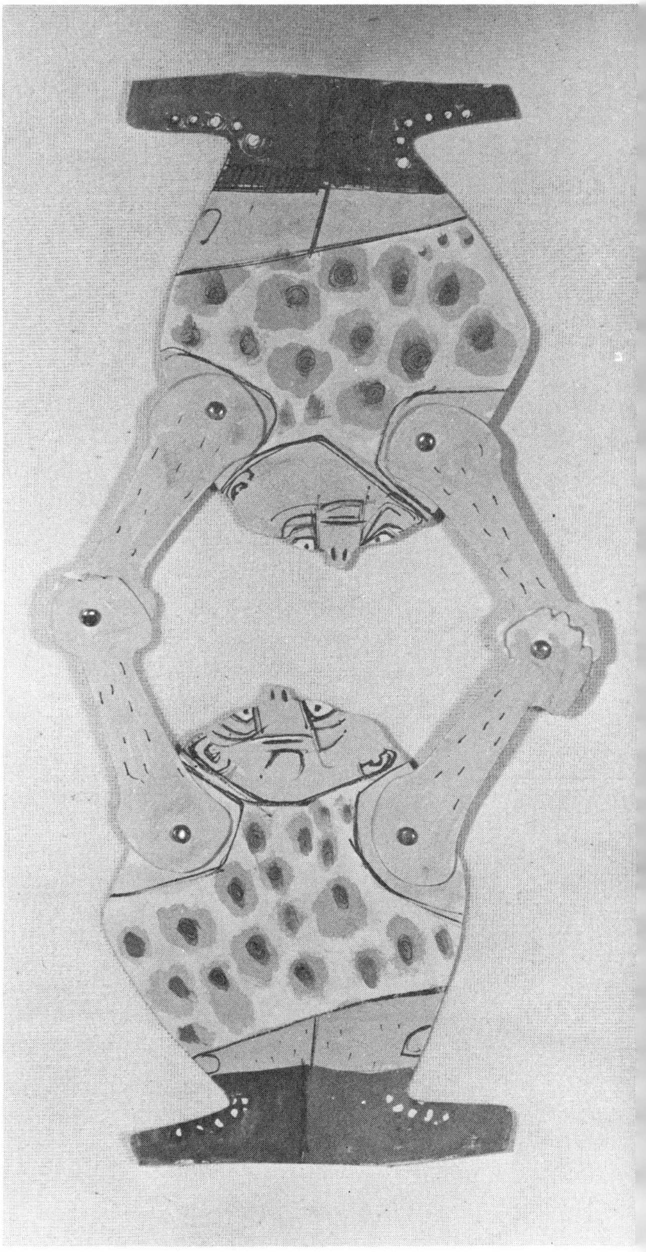

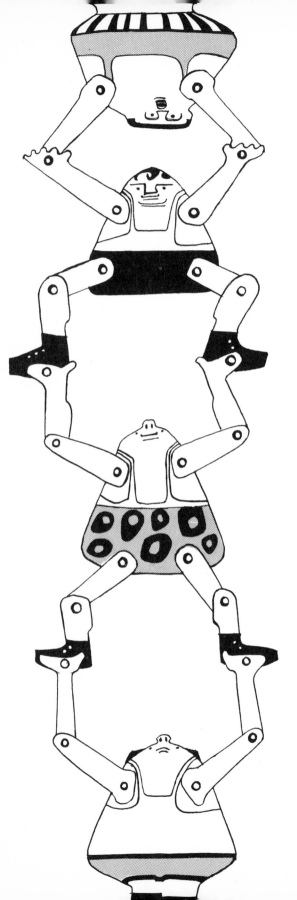

Fig. 81 The articulated toys can be developed in more ambitious arrangements

You will discover, if you make a version of the figures, that they can not only be moved up and down but they can also be rotated through a variety of weird and unpredictable movements. Although they are fixed at the hands they can actually be made to stand next to each other, still holding hands.

You can move them so that one is lying sideways and the other standing upright. You can make them touch noses, or make one stand behind the other.

This is a simple exercise but it can be visually attractive, and it is only intended as a toy. You might make one as a present for a younger brother or sister.

When you make articulated figures as simple toys, the choice of acrobats or other circus performers as a subject is obviously a good one. It might be interesting for a group of you to work together and see how many figures you can join by this method. If you start with approximately the same size cardboard for the bodies and for the arm pieces, it should be possible to fit a number of figures together and still retain the telescopic effect.

In the illustration (Fig. 81) a slightly more complex method of jointing is suggested. You will see that instead of the one-piece arms of the previous acrobats, some of these figures have the arms in two pieces, jointed at the elbows. This is the sort of development you can obviously try if you feel able to cope with it.

The articulated 'up and down' figures can be developed in other ways to make toys on different themes. There are other positions in which the parts can be assembled.

The diagram (Fig. 82) is an illustration of an alternative method of assembly. Two main body shapes are again used, but this time they are joined so that they can appear to be facing one another. This type of articulation will result in a different movement, which might suggest different subject matters.

The wrestlers (Fig. 83) are developed on this basis. If you watch people actually wrestling, especially the professionals, you might be astonished at the complicated and grotesque positions which they actually assume. With two figures articulated in this way you can do something similar. You can move them

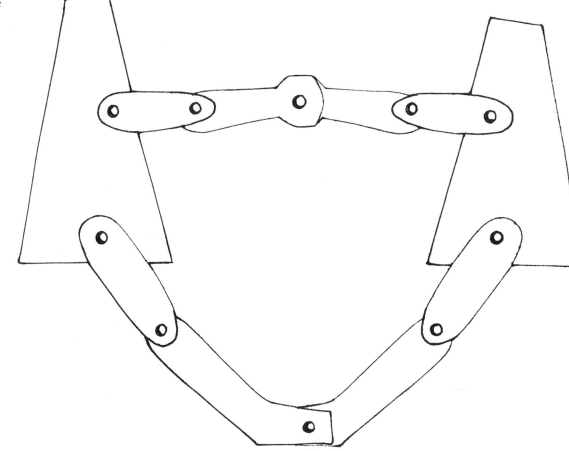

Fig. 82 Experiments can be made in different spacing and fixing of the figures.

into a variety of erratic positions, but you should only do this on the articulation you have included. During the course of any movement you should not break or open any of the points at which the figures are joined. All of the movement potential is included in the figures as you have made them. It should be fluent and continuous as you play with the toy.

If you discover a limitation, or if you want a movement which is not possible, you must investigate alternative methods of joining the figures. There are many more possibilities than those illustrated.

The wrestling figures can of course be made as different basic shapes. They do not have to have pear-shaped bodies or bullet heads as in the illustration. You can make the figures in any shape. The visual

Fig. 83 The movement potential of articulated groups can be supported with appropriate decorative treatments.

effect of anything you do can be very different from the illustrations, although you can use the techniques they describe.

The illustration (Fig. 84) shows the same method used on an alternative subject with more pattern potential. Instead of the wrestlers the two figures jointed in this way could suggest a dancing couple, which would be a good opportunity for some work with bright colours.

Your own version of the dancing couple might make an acceptable present for your parents—or even your grandparents—especially if you have included some special characteristics so that they are able to see something of themselves in the figures.

For other subjects you could think about any situation with figures struggling or making a combined sort of movement. You could have Indians fighting, or pairs of skaters. If you understand the basic idea you will be able to develop the toys in your own particular style.

Jumping Jacks

The articulated figures which have been described so far have all been examples in which you must hold the figures as you move them. There are other types of figure in which the movement can be operated from a remote control.

The best known example of the figure operated from a simple remote control is the Jumping Jack. This is more complex than the figures previously illustrated because it involves a simple mechanism.

The principle is illustrated in the diagram (Fig. 85), which shows the back view of the Jumping Jack. The normal Jack is made up of nine pieces: a body and head cut together in one piece, with a further two pieces for each of the arms and legs. These are in each case articulated at the knee or elbow, and where the limb is attached to the body.

If you consider the Jack without the operating strings, you will see that it has a similarity to the Marionette Figure. In this case also the joints should all be loose enough to allow a very free movement of the limbs. Whenever they are raised the lower section

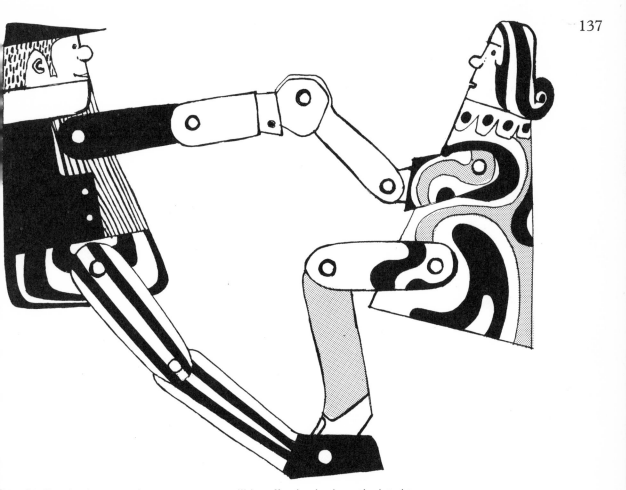

Fig. 84 Simple shapes and strong patterns will be effective in the articulated toys.

should hang vertically, and when they are dropped the whole limb should drop back into the position illustrated.

This is an essential principle of the Jumping Jack—that a mechanism can be used to raise the arms and legs, but that they will return freely to their original positions.

If they are made in fairly thick cardboard the Jacks can be large, possibly up to three times the height of this page. The main requirement with the cardboard you use is that it should not bow or bend, otherwise the movement which you have got through careful work with the paper fasteners will be restricted.

If you have never made and strung a Jack before, the following stringing method should make it a simple operation.

Legs

Make a hole at the top of each thigh above the paper fastener.

Connect the two thighs together with a string across the body (Fig. 85) *a a*. The string should be tied so that it is just horizontal, neither too tight nor too loose, when the legs are in their original vertical position.

Test with your fingernail that by pulling downwards on the middle of the string the two legs will be raised. If the string is too loose the test will merely take up the slack. If it is too tight the legs will already be partly raised before you make the test.

Arms

Make a hole at the top of each arm above the paper fastener, and connect the arms together with a string in the same way as you have done with the legs *b b*. Test the movement of the arms also in the same way.

Operating String

When you are satisfied that the two horizontal strings are correctly placed, the operating string can be added. It can be tied at the top, to the centre of the horizontal string, and again at the centre of the lower string. There should be enough of this string to extend below the body *c*. It must be tightly tied to the other strings, so that when it is pulled it will pull them down together. This will activate both arms and legs (Fig. 86). When the string is released they will drop back into their original positions.

To the beginner this might look like a complicated procedure, but it is in fact a simple piece of engineering based on the principle of the limbs pivoting where they join the body. If the principle is understood, it is unlikely that the stringing will prove to be impossibly difficult for anyone.

Your Jumping Jacks can be decorated in a variety of ways (Fig. 87). They can be painted with appropriate styles of dress, or can be treated as fun decorations.

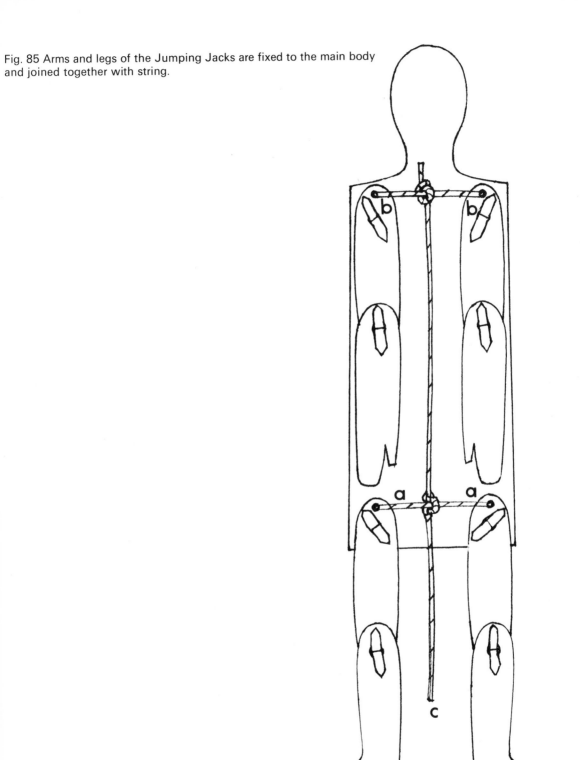

Fig. 85 Arms and legs of the Jumping Jacks are fixed to the main body and joined together with string.

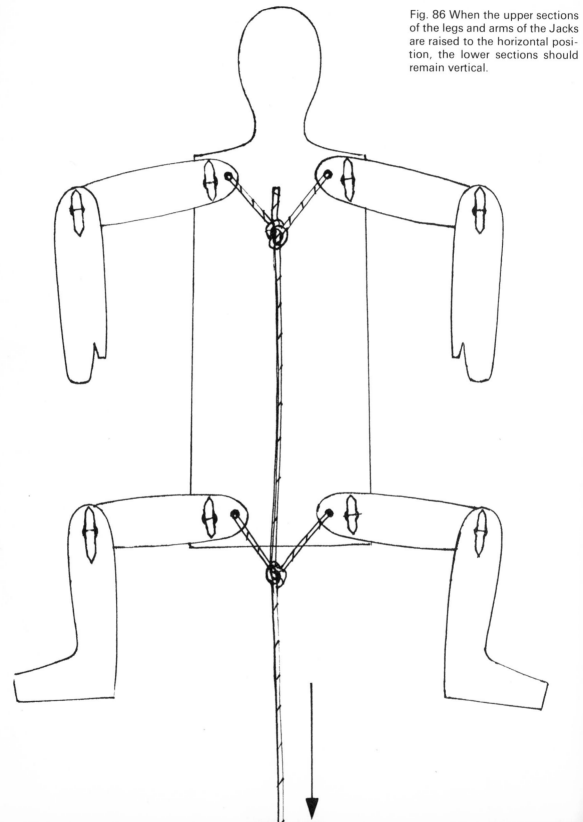

Fig. 86 When the upper sections of the legs and arms of the Jacks are raised to the horizontal position, the lower sections should remain vertical.

Fig. 87 Any type of figure can become a Jumping Jack.

A final piece of string can be fitted at the head if required, so that the Jacks can be hung as a decoration —waiting for someone to pull the string.

This is not a difficult toy to make, once you have mastered the stringing method. You will probably find that you will have to undo and retie the string at first, but this is usual. When you understand the principle, you should soon find yourself able to make Jumping Jacks which work smoothly when the strings are pulled.

It is a principle which can be applied to figures with a number of variations.

Hair Raisers

When you understand a principle which will allow certain types of modelling treatment, it is often possible to extend the principle and apply it in different ways in order to get different end effects.

If you can raise arms or legs on a figure, other models can be made to include, for example, raised hair or ears.

In the illustration (Fig. 88), simple head shapes are suggested with movement potential based on the Jumping Jack principle.

On the left side of the illustration you can see the back view of the faces. In each case additional features are suggested as shapes which pivot on paper fasteners. As you have seen, when these are joined above the pivot point with a horizontal string, a vertical string tied at the centre will make it possible for the features to be raised at the sides of the main shape. The results of pulling the strings are suggested in the front view of the faces.

You can see the visual effect of the method applied in this way in the clowns illustrated (Fig. 89). Before the hanging strings are pulled, they appear quite bald. When the string is pulled, appropriately shaped hair pieces are raised at the sides (Fig. 90).

These faces are made life-size and can be amusing if you place them when they are finished so that people —almost invariably inquisitive—will pull the hanging string. The hair-raising results might cause amusement at a party and add to the atmosphere, and even on an

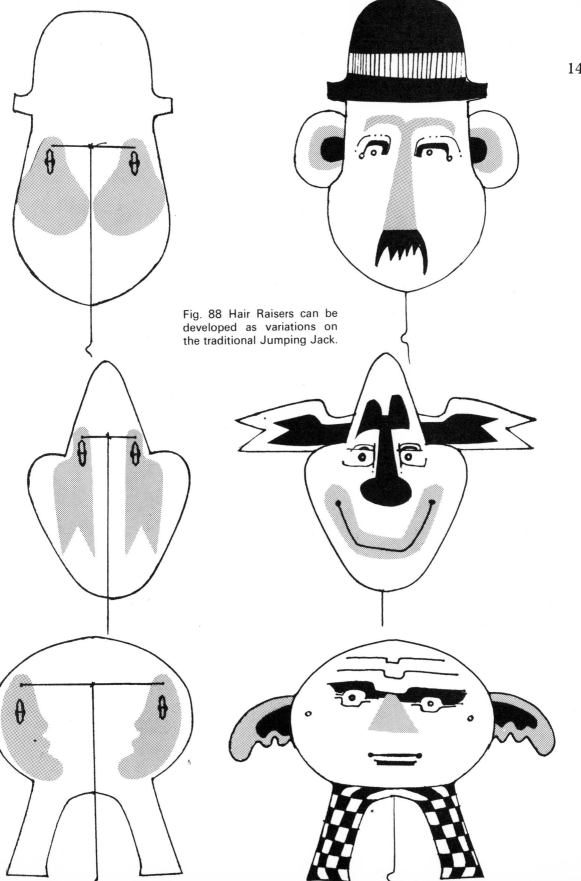

Fig. 88 Hair Raisers can be developed as variations on the traditional Jumping Jack.

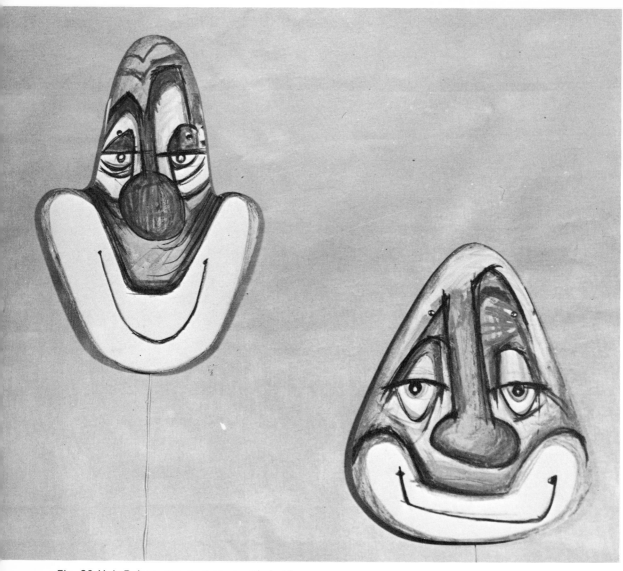

Fig. 89 Hair Raisers can start apparently bald.

ordinary day can brighten things up if you have an unsuspecting visitor.

Hair Raisers or fun faces based on the Jumping Jack principle can take other forms. You might experiment with faces with ears which can be raised and lowered. These might be made more effective by the addition of brightly coloured ear-rings, like the popular plastic ones with simple shapes in contrasting colours.

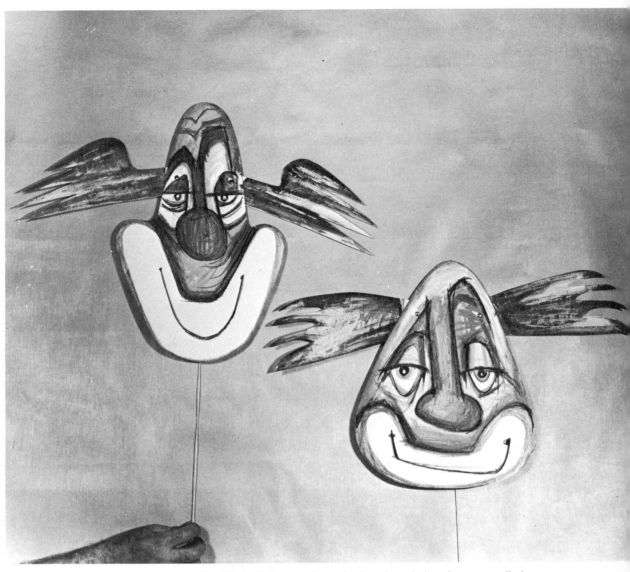

Fig. 90 And change dramatically when their strings are pulled.

On clowns, instead of hair, you might raise flowers or even flags. There are various possibilities which you might try.

In any attempt you make, you can develop the shape so that pulling the string will raise two or four pieces. The additions should be simple and bold and, if you can work it out, should be hidden out of sight behind the main shape until the string is pulled.

146   There is an opportunity with the Jumping Jacks, although in the main they will result in amusing toys, to give the work a slightly more serious intention.

In the same way as the legs and arms of a human figure can be moved, it is possible to mount the figure, and move the legs of the horse. This could be a light-hearted but useful extension to any work you might be doing as a support to your history studies.

The diagram (Fig. 91) illustrates a simple horse shape with a mounted figure included. There are five separate pieces to the assembly.

The main part a, which does not move, will form the body of the horse complete with rider. This part can also include the tail.

At the front, one section b can be made to include the neck and head of the horse with the upper part of the foreleg. This can be fixed with a paper fastener to the main body. It can have the lower leg also attached with a paper fastener.

The rear leg can be in two sections, upper and lower, also pivoted at the knee. It can be joined at a point on the body near the tail.

If you look closely at the diagram you should be able to make out the shapes described. If you have been able to cut and assemble something similar to the illustrated shape, and have fixed a horizontal string between the fore and back legs, dotted line c, the act of pulling this string should operate the model. The horse will raise its head and its legs at the pull. A continued raising and lowering of the string should convey the effect of the horse galloping.

The movement can be seen in the illustration (Fig. 92). If you compare the two shapes the difference in position of the head and legs caused by pulling the string can be seen.

If you have a reference book with suitable illustrations, you could dress the rider and decorate the horse according to the style of any period in which you are interested.

It might be interesting to make a number of mounted figures, and to suspend them with their strings attached to one operating bar, so that they could be made to move together like a troop of mounted soldiers.

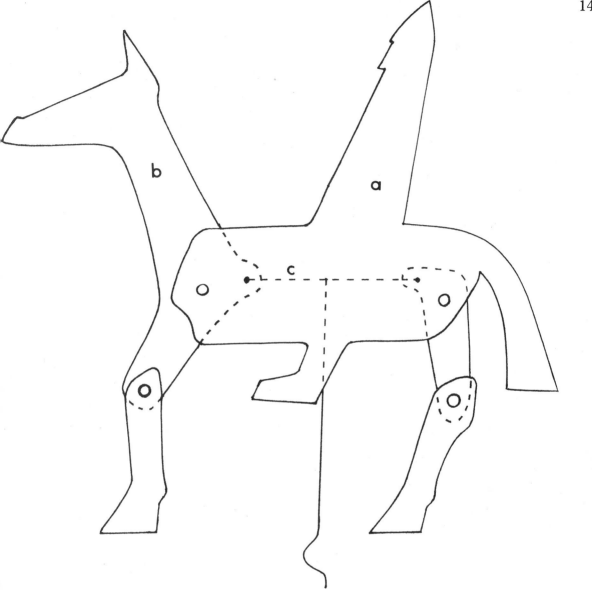

Fig. 91 A mounted figure can be made with a simple articulated technique included.

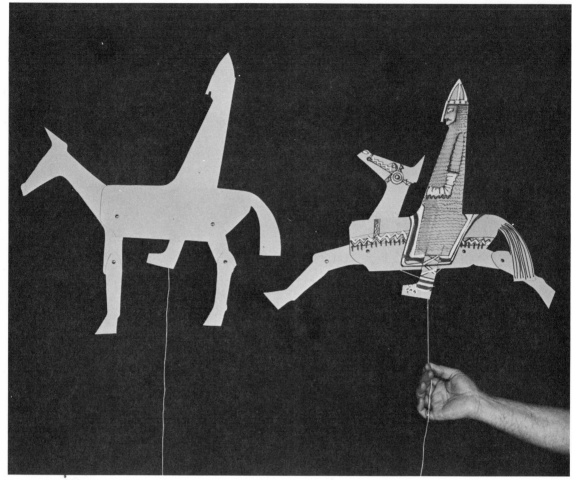

Fig. 92 The articulation of the mounted figure will result in a galloping movement when the string is operated.

If you have gained a measure of confidence in making Jumping Jacks or variations on the principle, there is a further interesting variation with amusing potential in the type of face which can be made to smile when the string is pulled.

This is a slightly more complex exercise, but if you study the diagrams carefully with the text, the Smilers should be no more difficult than any of the previous examples.

Smilers

In the diagram (Fig. 93) there are three separate shapes:

Section *a*—the nose and brow shape. You will need only ONE of these.

Section *b*—the cheek section. You will need TWO of these.

Section *c*—the chin and jaw section. You will need TWO of these.

If you feel uncertain of your ability to make the Smilers you could in this exercise actually take a tracing of the shapes before cutting them out.

After cutting the shapes you must place them together as in the diagram (Fig. 94), and fix them with paper fasteners at the points indicated.

The fixture at the centre top will be through three thicknesses of cardboard *a b b*.

The two sections *c* can be joined at the centre, and can be fixed at the sides to the lower parts of the two sections *b b*.

Fig. 93 Smilers can be assembled from basic shapes.

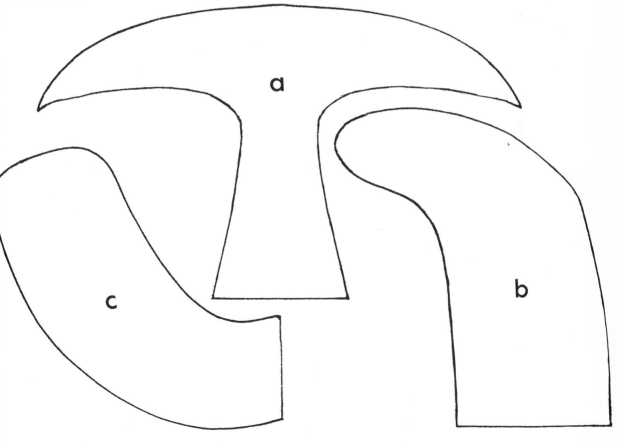

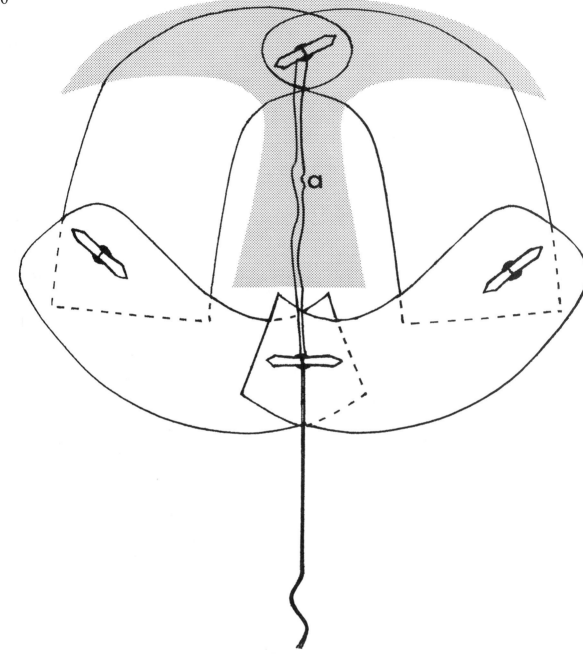

Fig. 94 When the basic shapes are fixed together a rubber band can be added between the two centre fasteners.

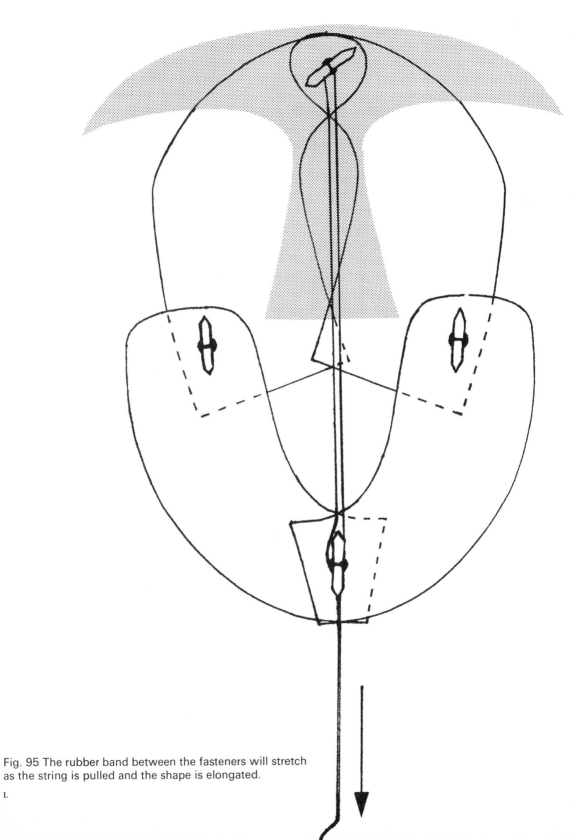

Fig. 95 The rubber band between the fasteners will stretch
as the string is pulled and the shape is elongated.

L

Fig. 96 The Smilers might start looking sad.

If you compare your work stage by stage with the diagrams, you should be able to resolve any problems in the construction. If you are in any doubt you can place the assembled shapes on the diagram in order to check that your assembly of the shapes is reasonably accurate.

When the five pieces are joined together it should be possible to hold the top in one hand while you move the chin up and down with the other. The result beneath the nose will be similar to the movement of a mouth opening and closing.

If the assembled shapes can be made to work in this way, a rubber band can be fixed at the back of the

shape from the top centre fastener to the bottom one (Fig. 94) *a*. The rubber band should be slightly loose when the shapes are assembled in the position shown in the diagram.

When the rubber band is in place it should be stretched tight by the movement of opening the mouth in the assembly. When it is released, the tension should cause the mouth to close. A string can be added to the bottom fastener so that pulling is made easy (Fig. 95).

This diagram illustrates what should happen to the assembled shapes when the string is pulled. The whole structure will be elongated, and the opening under the nose will appear. The rubber band will also be stretched tight.

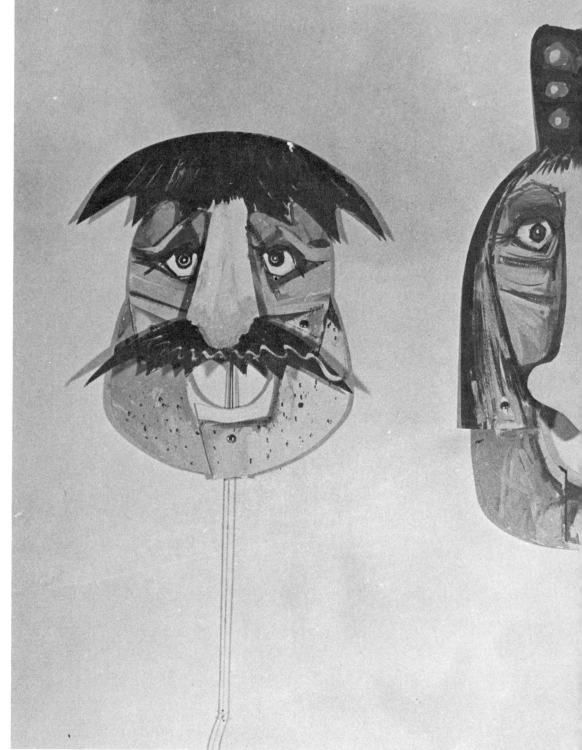

Fig. 97 They might liven up when their strings are pulled.

If you have made your first Smiler from the diagrams it will be smaller than the shape has to be, but you can still complete it with eyes and features at the front.

When you have understood the way the Smilers work, you can develop more of them on a larger scale, with particular features which you can decide on and include for yourself.

The examples (Fig. 96) illustrate some ways in which Smilers might be developed. In this illustration the faces are in their original assembled positions. The same faces are shown in the next illustration, with strings pulled and the elastic stretched. (Fig. 97). In the example on the right you will see the original face, illustrated by the shapes in the construction diagrams, with a bun of hair included on the head and nose shape. The other examples include different simple developments.

Whether the characters really smile when their strings are pulled may not be too obvious in any Smilers you produce. But the act of pulling the strings will certainly change the appearance of the faces, and will communicate some sort of human process. The result might be a smile, or it might be a toothless grin.

This is again an exercise which you can make and hang for the benefit of the inquisitive. Watching their reactions as they pull the strings and make the Smilers work might give you as much pleasure as making and operating them yourself.

When you have been making some of the various types of articulated figures, you have really been making toys. These are very simple and inexpensive toys, but they can still cause amusement and pleasure when they are played with. There are other simple toys which can be based on figures and which can be made in cardboard.

Spinners This exercise is really only an opportunity to paint
and draw faces on a shape which becomes interesting
when you make it perform a simple movement.

The Spinner is an old-fashioned toy, based on a
circular-shaped piece of cardboard which is made to
spin on a doubled string. In spite of its simplicity
it will have one quality which no other exercise in
this book will have. The Spinners can be made as
faces and, according to various treatments which you
give them, these faces will have the ability to make
their own particular noises.

You must begin with a circle of cardboard. It should
be fairly stiff, so that the circle will not bow out of
shape when you decorate it.

A loop of string must be threaded through the card
from one side, and back through it from the other.
When it is tied in the loop it should be long enough
so that it can be held between the hands when your
arms are extended straight out from the body. You
should not make the loop so long that your arms must
be stretched at the sides to make it taut.

The knot of the loop should be at one of the ends,
where it is held, and not close to the disc.

When you spin the disc you will find it possible,
by a gentle and continuous process of bringing your
arms together and then opening them, to keep and
increase a fluent and non-stop rate of spin.

As your arms come together the string will wind on
itself. As you extend your arms the string will unwind,
and rotate the disc.

This movement, which can make the disc spin very
rapidly, will tend to saw through the card where the
holes are positioned closely together, as they must be.
In order to eliminate this cutting and to make the
Spinner last any length of time, you must stick
strengthening pieces on both sides of the disc before
piercing the holes for the string.

In the diagram (Fig. 98) the Spinner is illustrated
at a suitable size, with the toned area indicating the
attached strengthening piece. You should pay particular attention to the distance between the holes.

There might be some trial and error stages necessary
when you start making Spinners, before you can get
the holes exactly right. If they are too far apart, the

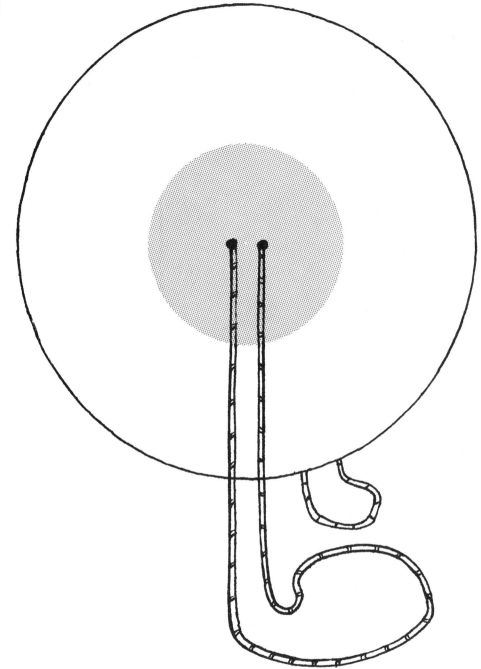

Fig. 98 The Spinner must have strengthening discs on both sides at the centre.

Fig. 99 Spinners can be made with faces painted decoratively on the surface and with edge cut treatments for sound effects.

shape will not spin because the disc will have too much sideways movement on the loop. If they are too close they will quickly merge into one large hole.

Spinners can be decorated with a variety of simple faces (Fig. 99). The added strengthening pieces at the centre might sometimes be made into a nose, which might help to keep the features simple.

In the illustration you can see the way the strings tend to curl up when the Spinners have been used. This makes them much easier to spin subsequently.

You will also see that in some of them various parts have been cut from the edges. In others, holes have been punched into the discs. This treatment, which has many possible variations, will cause the Spinners to make a high-pitched sound when they are operated.

You can experiment with this sound effect, trying to discover ways of giving your Spinners particularly effective sound qualities. A group of you working with Spinners can, in fact, make a great deal of noise. But this obviously cannot be described. If you are interested you will make the Spinners, so that you can make the noise—and listen.

There is another interesting aspect to the Spinners. This is the aspect of colour change which takes place as the discs spin. After painting and decorating them with colour you will find that interesting variations in tone and colour will occur as you spin them.

There are reasons for these changes, as there are reasons for the changes which occur in any process of colour mixing. When you begin to be aware of the reasons you will be able to work out and control the changing results of the spinning. You might, in fact, find it possible to mix colour by optical effect, rather than by putting actual pigments together as a mixture. It might be another interesting field for you to start researching.

Swingers

Like the Spinners, this is another long established and fairly simple toy. It is cheap and easy to make, and has a quite remarkable movement potential.

The idea of the Swinger is that a simple cardboard figure can be made to do a variety of exercises on a type of trapeze.

In the diagram (Fig. 100) you will see that the body of the figure is a flat piece of cardboard with a round hole cut through it at the armpit.

A *U*-shaped arm section is inserted through this hole so that the body hangs from its upper edge. If you look at the diagram closely you will see that the figure of the Swinger is attached only at this point, although the arms are attached to strings at the top.

The diameter of the hole in the body should be slightly larger than the width of the arm section at the lowest point of the *U*, where it touches the body. The arms themselves, of course, cannot be wider at any point than the diameter of the hole, otherwise you will not be able to pass the arm through the body.

If you cut the arm section—with the arms parallel as illustrated—and insert it through the body, you can pause at this stage to test the movement.

If you start with the armpiece vertical, holding it at the top, when you raise the arm to a horizontal position, the figure should still hang vertically. If the figure goes up horizontally with the arms, the point where the two sections touch is fitted too tightly. There must be a small clearance at the fixture, and if it is too tight you might need to cut a sliver from the bottom of the arm section.

Your test is simple at this stage. When the arms are hanging down, the body must also be hanging down. When the arms are raised to the horizontal—compare the right-hand figure in the illustration (Fig. 102)—the body must still be hanging down.

If your Swinger is satisfactory at this stage, you can go on to the assembly.

For the next stage you must thread through the tops of the arms, and must fix the thread at both sides to a wooden rod.

In the diagram (Fig. 100) the Swinger is fixed to two lengths of round section dowel. This is separated immediately below the figure by a distance piece. This can be a piece of flat section timber drilled with holes the same size as the dowel.

You should be able to see that unless the dowels are held in something like this distance piece, they will flop around in any direction.

The arrows in the diagram illustrate the point where

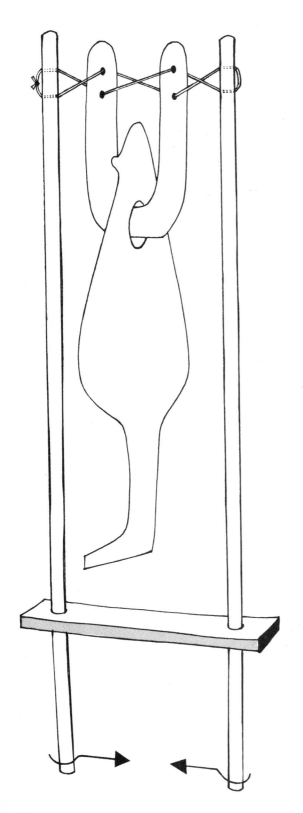

Fig. 100 The Swinger has a simple body shape with the arm section inserted through a hole at the shoulder.

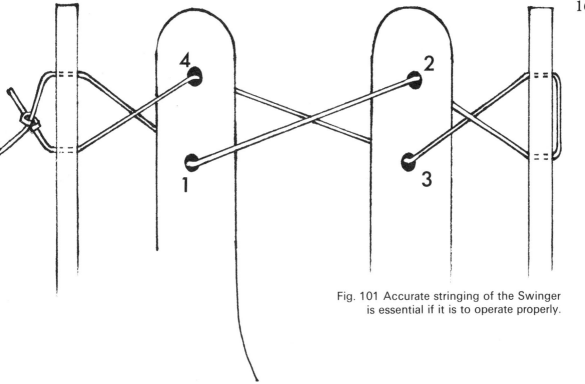

Fig. 101 Accurate stringing of the Swinger
is essential if it is to operate properly.

a slight inward pressure on the dowel will raise the Swinger into a variety of positions. This is illustrated again in Fig. 102.

The movement of the Swinger will be caused by a tightening and loosening of the threads at the top of the arms. Since this threading must be done with precision it is illustrated separately (Fig. 101).

After drilling holes in your dowel, for which you will need a very small drill in a hand brace, you must start threading at the top left-hand point. Before you start the threading you must have two holes, as illustrated, in each of the dowels.

Threading from the top you will go from back to front through the hole *1*, up and across to *2*, and through it from the front.

From hole *2* you must thread through the lower hole in the dowel, from the inner to the outside.

Inserting the thread back through the upper hole, it must cross BEHIND the one already there, and must enter hole *3* from the front.

Emerging from the back of hole *3*, your thread must

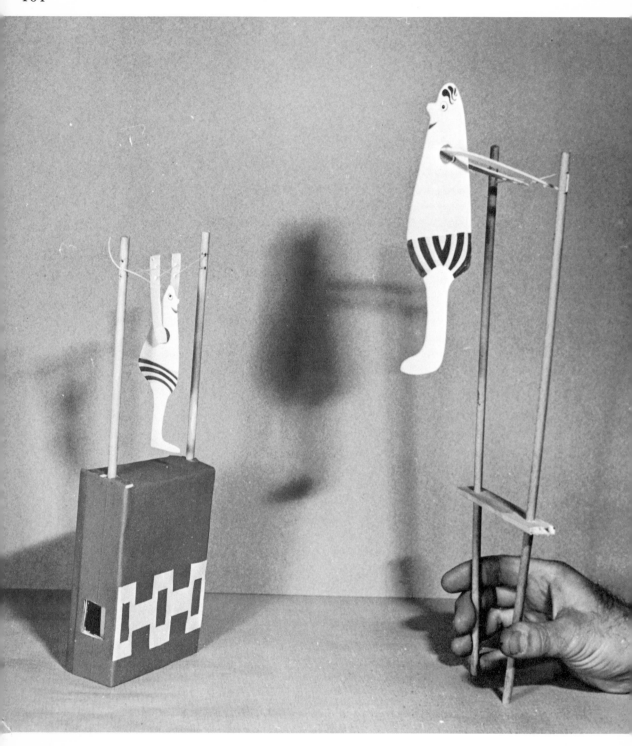

Fig. 102 Swingers can be made in various sizes, as a hand toy or as a free standing model.

again cross BEHIND the existing thread, and must enter hole *4* from the back.

Emerging from the front of hole *4* the thread will cross IN FRONT of the first thread into the lower hole in the first dowel.

When this thread is through the dowel and pulled tight at every point so that although it is not pulling the dowels together it is not hanging slack anywhere, it can be tied off at the side.

The accurate threading of the arms is essential if the Swinger is to work, but it should not be difficult if you follow the instructions stage by stage, and check your work against them as you go along.

An alternative method of keeping the dowels separate is to use a suitably sized box (Fig. 102). The box, which should be of cardboard, can have small holes cut in the sides at the top so that the dowels can be inserted into them.

A further hole cut in one side of the box as illustrated will allow you to put the necessary inward pressure on the lower part of the dowel. This is only necessary on one side.

The box itself can be decorated as well as the figure. Its use instead of the wooden distance piece has the advantage of making the toy a free-standing decoration when it is not being played with.

Swingers are not difficult to make. The process might at first look more complicated than it actually is. But when you have made one which can be operated to swing itself up and down, and even in complete somersaults, you will probably be able to make others without even having to look back at the diagrams.

Jack in the Box   When you have been successful with some of the toys made in cardboard, you might try inventing others for yourself or developing in this material toys you already know.

Like the Spinners and Swingers the Jack in the Box is a long-established toy. It is a very simple toy which is now much less common than it used to be. There might even be some people who have never experienced it.

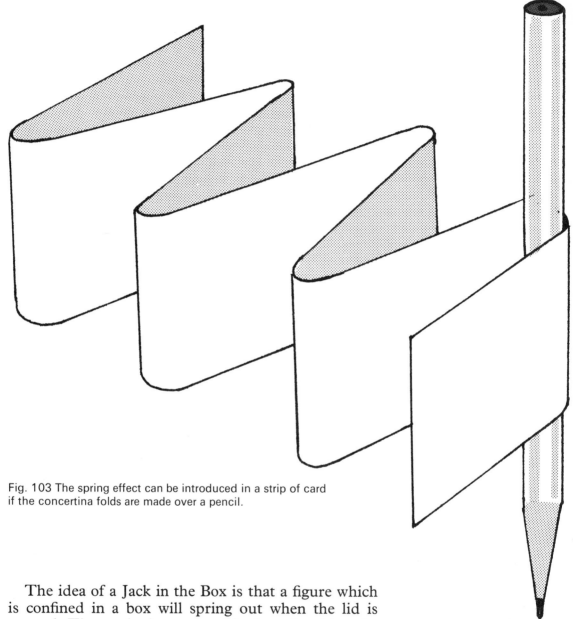

Fig. 103 The spring effect can be introduced in a strip of card
if the concertina folds are made over a pencil.

The idea of a Jack in the Box is that a figure which
is confined in a box will spring out when the lid is
opened. The method most used is that of making the
figure with a cover over a thin metal spring.

It is interesting to see, however, that if you con-
certina-fold a long strip of cardboard, it will have a
tendency to spring open. You can help this tendency
when you are making the concertina, if you make your
folds curved over a pencil, rather than sharply folded
(Fig. 103).

Sharp folds, which are pressed together so that the surface of the card is fractured, will prevent a good springing quality in the card, but the rounded fold, which will allow the card to be pressed into a box, will actually make it possible to develop the Jack in the Box entirely in cardboard.

After making the concertina fold in a long thin strip of card, one end can be cut as a head, and the other can be gummed to the inside base of a box.

The box should be made to fit the folded strip. It should be slightly larger than the width of the strips and the width of the folds, so that, when it is opened, the strip will spring out freely without being held back by being too tightly fitted.

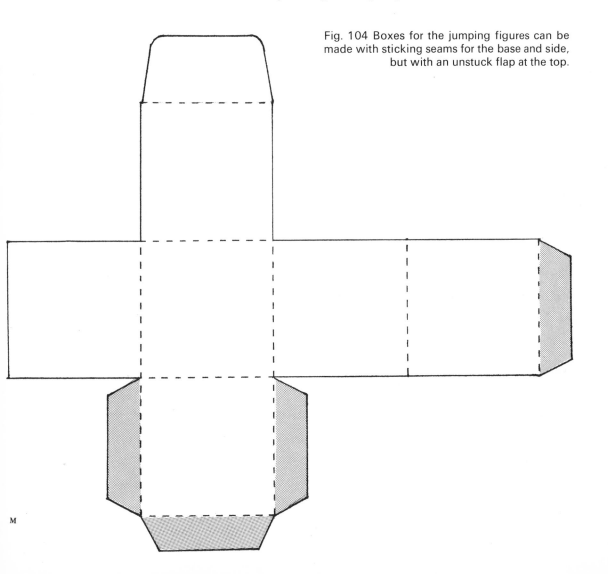

Fig. 104 Boxes for the jumping figures can be made with sticking seams for the base and side, but with an unstuck flap at the top.

M

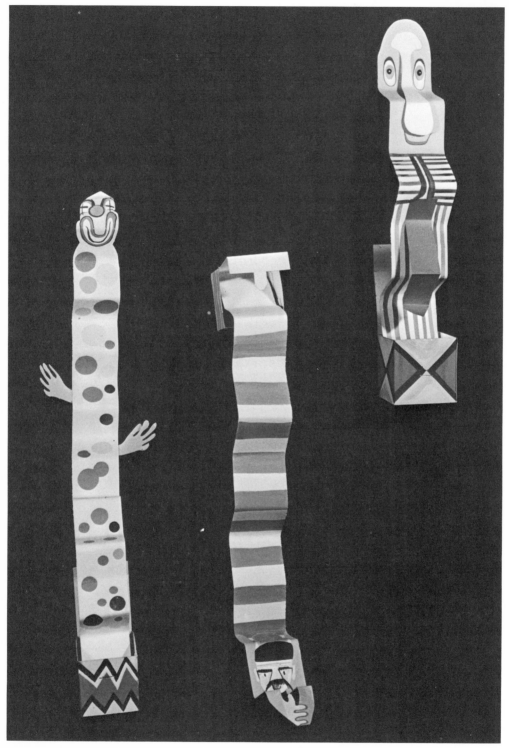

Fig. 105 A cardboard Jack in the Box is possible in a variety of shapes.

To make a box you will need to make an opened cube with sticking seams. If you are not sure of the method, the diagram (Fig. 104) shows one possible arrangement of the sides of the cube, with sticking seams shown as toned areas. These must be gummed when the box is made up.

The dotted lines indicate points at which you must score the cardboard so that the edges of the box are precise. The large flap on the top square in the diagram is not stuck. This is the tuck-in flap which will hold the lid closed.

In the finished examples (Fig. 105) differences have been introduced into the figures. The clown has paper hands which can be folded in when the box is closed on the figure. The figure on the right has an added nose in thin paper, which can also be folded in as well as the tie. The centre figure, instead of jumping, appears to be diving out of the box.

It is of course not possible to make these with as much spring as the normal Jack in the Box, but if you experiment with them you should be able to get enough spring in the card to frighten anyone opening the boxes.

It is useful to remember that when the box is not in use the lid should be left open, and the strip should be out of the box. This will help to retain the maximum springing potential in it when it is folded.

The Jack in the Box is another example of a figure in cardboard which can be made as a toy, and can be used as a decoration. Both the Jack and the Box should be as gay and colourful as you can make them, with the simple sort of pattern and decorative treatment which has immediate visual appeal.

Up and Down Faces

There is a final and very simple toy which you might like to make as a relaxation from some of the earlier more demanding exercises.

These are merely faces, which you can pin to the wall or which you might like to send to your friends. The Up and Down face is a very old trick.

If you look at the illustration (Fig. 106) you will see a row of benevolent and smiling faces. These are

Fig. 106 Up and Down Faces can reflect very different moods.

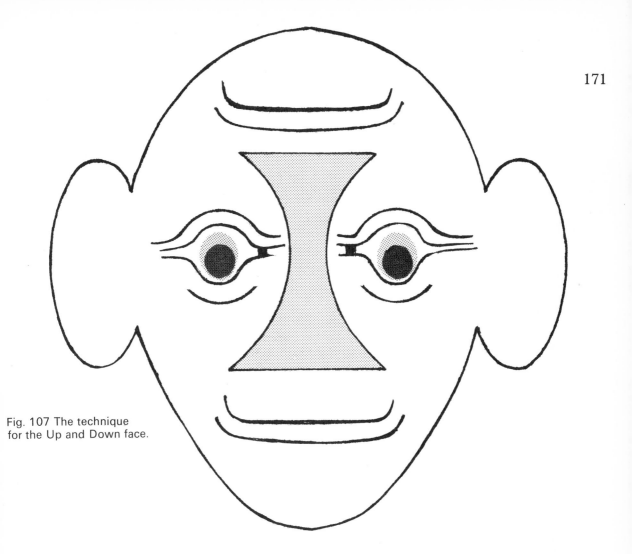

Fig. 107 The technique
for the Up and Down face.

just painted on cardboard. They are happy faces. You
could make some in the likenesses of some of your
friends or relatives.

Now turn the book upside down. The faces have
changed their moods, and some have changed their
total appearance.

There is nothing profound or important about this
toy. The trick which causes the change in mood was
often used in the past, but is seen less and less today.

The technique of the changing mood is illustrated
in the diagram (Fig. 107). On any oval or rounded face
you should make a nose which does not have any
clearly identifiable top or bottom.

Eyes can be added to the face as close to the middle
as possible so that there is a similar amount of space
above and below them.

For the smiling face the mouth is defined with an upward curve.

For the frowning face the mouth must curve downwards.

You will notice that when it is not serving as a mouth, either of the curves will act as a wrinkled forehead.

This is a simple trick which can be developed in various ways. A beard on one aspect of the face will become hair when the shape is reversed. A lady with a bun might even become a man with a beard. It is a simple and old-fashioned piece of fun, which might cause some interested reaction.

If you could persuade your teacher to let you have a row of these pinned to the wall, perhaps in the likeness of everyone in the class, you could reflect the mood of the class. If they were pinned through the centre it would be a simple operation to change them round according to currently successful—or less happy—pieces of work or performance. If you were all working well it would be very nice for your teacher to see so many smiling faces, both in the flesh and on the wall.

Masks

After the Up and Down faces, which are intended merely to be pinned to the wall, it is a simple step to making faces which can be worn.

You might have seen that the Up and Down faces could have been pierced at the eyes and could have been used as simple masks. There is a lot of fun to be had from mask making, but like any work in a craft the fun will have more potential for extension and development if there is an understanding on the part of the craftsman.

You might have seen this in previous exercises in which, in order to arrive at certain visual effects, you worked on a basic shape. The basic shape was a starting point or foundation on which to build, and when it was established, it eliminated some of the earlier and more tiresome problems of how something might be done. After eliminating the problems it acted as a support for the more creative processes, or for the fun.

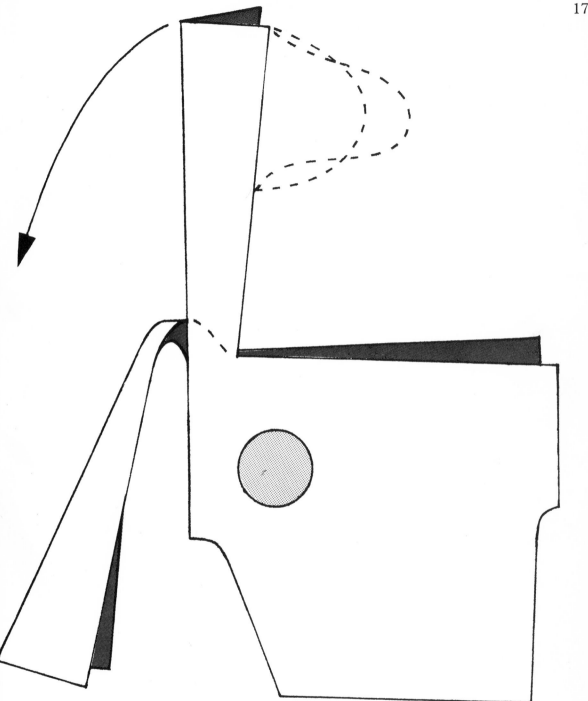

Fig. 108 A basic shape for masks can be cut on the fold, with a nose included at the top.

If you look at the question of masks, you will see that all of them will have certain things in common. If you can see these characteristics you will be able to arrive at a basic shape.

A mask in cardboard must stretch across the face, and will probably need a section cut away to make a bridge at the wearer's nose. It will have holes properly placed so that they can be looked through. If it is to represent the human face it will have a nose as the foremost projection.

These are basic and almost inevitable characteristics, and it should be possible to combine them into one basic shape.

A suggested example is illustrated in the diagram (Fig. 108). The shape can be cut symmetrical on the fold. In the diagram the basic shape is illustrated in two stages. If you place your hand over the nose shape at the left of the diagram, you will see how the mask can be cut with the nose included at the top.

If you remove your hand and place it now over the extension at the top, you will see how this shape can be folded down to make the nose at the front of the mask, which is how it will be worn.

The dotted lines at the top of the mask illustrate various alternative shapes for the nose. You will be able to think of more of these.

The basic shape is illustrated in the top left-hand example in Fig. 109. This can be developed or added to in a variety of ways. You might try the shape with painted decoration, hair—straight or curled, moustaches and whiskers, or ear-rings.

You might add brightly patterned ties (Fig. 110), which could be cut separately and stapled or gummed to the nose. If you use staples in the construction of a mask, some care must be taken to cover any sharp points which can tangle in the hair or scratch the skin. Gummed strip or adhesive tape can be used over any staples which might make wearing the mask uncomfortable.

There are various methods of fixing masks so that they can be worn. String, for going round the head, can be fixed at the sides, or rubber bands which can be worn over the ears. With any fixture it will be necessary to strengthen the mask with added stuck

Fig. 109 Development of the basic mask shape can include a variety of cut and painted treatments.

Fig. 110 Boldly patterned additions can be made to the basic mask.

paper where the fastening is added. If this is not done it will not be possible to make the mask adequately secure when it is worn without the likelihood of tearing the basic shape.

Masks can be used as decorations for almost any occasion. If you have made them on the fold it will be possible to pin them up with a measure of form projecting forwards. This will be emphasized by the nose and by any added features.

There are of course other forms which can be developed as masks. You can make a simple rectangle or oval with holes for the eyes, and can add the nose afterwards. This would involve a more economical use of paper than the method illustrated.

Another mask could cover the face completely, and could be cut with a chin included. This might be more effective visually, but could be a disadvantage at a party where the wearer was going to eat or drink. It might also prove to be a disadvantage in a performance when the wearer was expected to talk.

When you are making masks you will be helped by having a basic shape to rely on. You will also be helped by understanding that the mask is not intended to be an accurate representation of the human face. When it is painted it is not necessary to make a careful blending of tones of pink. The mask can be in any colours to suit the effect you want, and it is best when treated with a formal pattern rather than painted naturalistically.

Masks are fun to make, and can be impressive as decorations. The examples illustrated are only a beginning. For the rest of your work you should look at people, and should then try to interpret them in your own way. You can make a whole variety of masks if you understand a basic shape and can exploit it in your own particular method and style.

Decorations   You will have noticed in many of the exercises you have already attempted the recurring suggestion that the figures or faces you have made might be used as decorations.

There are many occasions to which a decoration can add something, if it is well made and visually acceptable. There are parties and special times of the year, and other special occasions like homecomings from hospital.

In schools there are open and prize days, sales to raise funds, and public performances of plays.

In clubs there are special fun nights and gala occasions. They are all potential opportunities for decorations. And because of the cheap and less durable nature of the materials you have been using they are eminently suitable for decorations.

When they are used, decorations change an environment in some way, and it is obvious that the change should be a gay and improving one. This was considered in one of the earlier exercises. Attractive colours and simple shapes are essential, but with the brightest colours and simplest shapes there are still many possible opportunities to base decorations on people and faces. People can in fact be very decorative and very amusing.

Target Figures

If you can imagine walking into a room or into a hall where there are hanging lots of large circles in the brightest possible colours, you may have some idea of the effect of a decoration with Target Figures.

These are simple fun figures which can be hung, and each of which has a large target-like shape in the middle. The target can be boldly patterned. This is what will make the impact in the decoration. The rest of the figure should be very simple in shape, and need not be more than a very basic statement of the figure—head, body and legs. This also can be simply patterned (Fig. 111).

Target Figures should be made with cardboard. If, however, you do not have enough available, you might make the targets from card and the rest of the figures from paper. Since you will be decorating the figures with paint or with stuck decoration, the targets could be made with card salvaged from large cartons.

If the Target Figures are going to be pinned against a wall they can be life-size. If they are to be hung their size will obviously depend on the amount of space below the ceiling.

Decorations are usually most satisfactory when they are out of reach. There is always a temptation for someone to touch and pull them if they are too low, and if they are made in paper this could obviously quickly ruin them.

If you make a number of Target Figures as decorations you will learn something about the art of preparing a decoration. It will not matter how many of them you make; there will be a factor which occurs throughout the decoration. This will be the emphatic round-shaped target which, seen over and over again, will be a key linking the whole effect into a unity. It is like a theme which becomes familiar and which

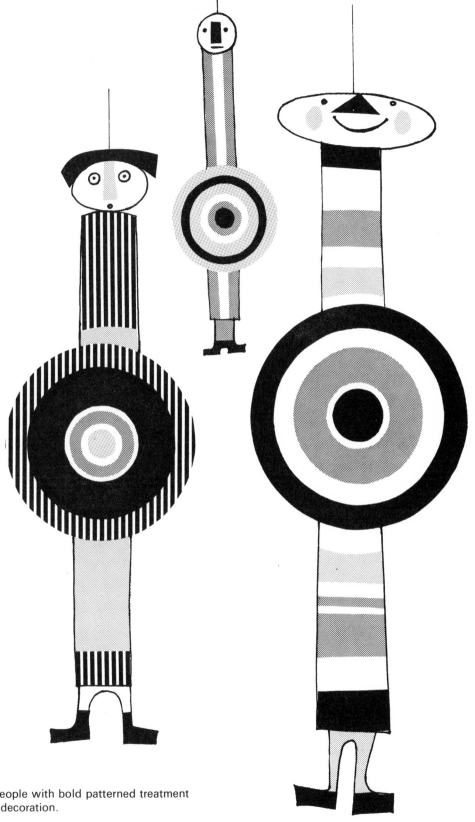

Fig. 111 Target People with bold patterned treatment can be used as a decoration.

we are happy with because we recognize it.

The same sort of happy repetition might occur in a decoration when a colour scheme is decided on and used.

You could imagine this in a decoration with Target Figures if the targets were all in warm colours for example—oranges and reds, or if the centre spot in every target was in the same colour.

Controlled colour does not mean that lots of bright and happy colours are not possible. It means that certain colours are chosen and used deliberately in order to hold the over-all effect together.

With a decoration of Target Figures it should not be difficult to decide on the colours you will use, and on the places where you will have your key colours.

Folded Faces

Party decorations are often produced from paper which is folded and then cut. When the paper is opened out each cut is reproduced as many times as the paper was folded, which applies also to the shapes made by the cuts.

You can probably remember doing something like this when you were very young. You might have taken a square of paper, folded it a number of times and then snipped at it with scissors. Afterwards, when you opened the paper out, you might have been intrigued at the pattern effect which you made with the cuts.

Using a simplified version of this technique, it is possible to produce and develop an interesting decoration based on a face shape which occurs over and over again.

The diagram (Fig. 112) illustrates a strip of paper concertina-folded a number of times.

In the lower example a semi-circular shape with an extension on the side illustrates the sort of cut which will make a Folded Face result. The centre of the circle is on the fold in the diagram, and the extension flap touches the narrow edges of the strip.

When this shape is cut, the toned areas will be removed. When the concertina strip is unfolded after cutting, the result will be a series of complete circles linked together with tabs. It is an ideal shape for faces

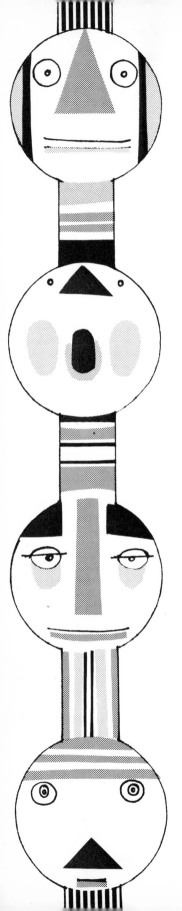

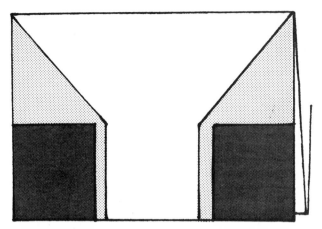

Fig.112 Folded Faces can be cut in a number of different shapes on concertina folds.

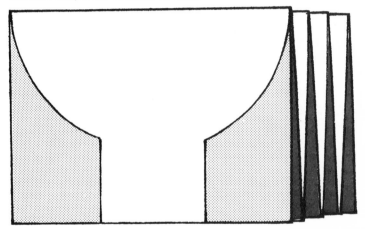

on the circles, separated in the finished effect with patterned tabs (Fig. 113).

Folded Faces can be made in paper, preferably of good quality so that it will take paint and added decoration. They do not have to be particularly large because it is not difficult to make a lot of them. The folding and cutting can be done very quickly, although the applied decoration will of course take longer.

In the upper example (Fig. 112) alternative methods of cutting are illustrated. If, after folding the strip, the darker shapes are cut away the resultant faces will be almost square. If the lighter area is removed they

Fig. 113 Folded Faces with simple features and bold patterns can form the basis of a decoration.

182   will be diamond-shaped. There are, as you will have seen, other alternatives to the examples illustrated, and you can investigate these for yourself.

You must begin with a long and narrow strip of paper, and you must concertina fold it into equal sized shapes. The easiest way to do this may be to fold the strip in two at the centre. Then to fold each of the two halves back on themselves so that you have three folds and four equal pieces.

If these are still too large you can fold the whole thing into half again, which will give you equally spaced folds, although if you do this you will have to open the folds and remake the concertina before cutting.

When you cut the Folded Faces it is desirable for visual effect that they should be symmetrical. So your cut should be the same on both sides of the strip. In this way you will discover some interesting and pleasing face shapes when you open the strip, which should make your Folded Faces very suitable for hanging as decorations.

You will probably be familiar with the type of expanding paper chains which can be bought as decorations, especially for use at Christmas. These are of the type which you can buy neatly folded, and which make patterns when they are opened out because the paper has been cut and stuck in certain ways. There is a simple technique involved in various ways in their manufacture. It is one which you can learn easily, and can use in making your own decorations.

Expanded Figures

Paper can be made to expand or grow larger by certain methods of folding and cutting. You can investigate this by taking a strip of fairly thin paper, about as wide as this page but longer if possible, and folding it longways through the centre.

After folding the paper, you must cut it with a series of parallel cuts across the folded width. You must make these cuts at regular intervals from the fold to the outer edge, but stopping short of the edge at the same distance with each cut.

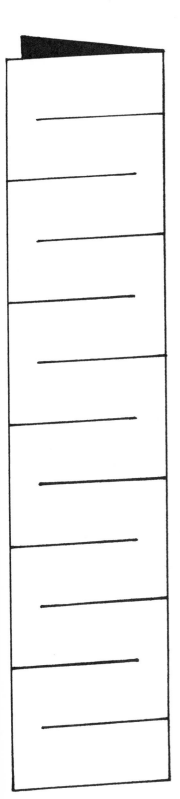

A second series of cuts can then be made, also across the width, from the outer edge to the fold, and again stopping short at the same distance from the fold. This is illustrated in the diagram (Fig. 114). The cuts are evenly spaced, and you should be able to do this by eye, although if you prefer you can measure before cutting.

After making the two rows of cuts you can open the paper out flat, noting its normal length. If you now pull it gently from both ends it will expand, and will form an interesting pattern between the cuts.

It might be necessary to practise this before you can judge the most suitable distance between the cuts, but when you can make paper expand neatly you can use the technique.

If you start with a piece of coloured paper—the larger the better—and you cut and expand it, you can use it for the body of a decorative clown.

You can draw round your own hand to make hands in contrasting colour, which can be stuck to the expanded paper. You can also add feet and a head (Fig. 115), or any other feature which will add to the decorative effect. As decorations the Expanded Figures can be pinned to the wall or can be hung from a single strand of cotton so that they rotate slowly.

A variation on the Expanded Figure can be made by cutting an actual figure shape, which can be as simple as possible, and making the expanding cuts in the body (Fig. 116). When you make these cuts you will not touch the arms or legs of the figure.

If you use this method you might find it necessary sometimes to add extra length to the arms when the figure is expanded. Otherwise, if the paper expands to any length, the original arms might seem disproportionately short.

Ties and moustaches, and other decorative features, can be added to these Expanded Figures, but you must try to avoid hiding the pattern made with the cuts. This pattern can be varied from figure to figure by using a different space between the cuts, which will make a further visually interesting factor in a decoration (Fig. 117).

Fig. 114 The cuts for Expanded Figures must be at regular intervals on opposite sides of the folded paper.

Fig.115 Faces, hands and feet can be added to lengths of expanded paper to make decorative figures.

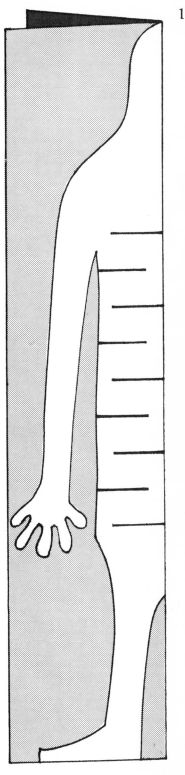

Fig. 116 When a figure is cut on the
fold the body can be cut to expand.

186

Fig. 117 Different spaces between the cuts on the bodies will result in different visual effects in the Expanded Figures.

A more complex method of expanding paper can be investigated by folding the paper twice along its length before cutting, although for simple and effective Expanding Figures the single fold is quite adequate.

Hanging Faces   If you have been working on the hanging figures as
decorations you might have seen that there are
ways of making decorations by hanging faces without
bodies.

If you were to draw a portrait on a rectangle of
paper, you would not find it unreasonable to pin
the drawing to the wall, even though it was without
a body.

If you were to cut out the face from the background
you might wear it as a mask, and instead of remaining
fixed it would move as you moved your head. It
seems a natural step to remove the mask and to suspend
it, so that like a face in real life, it will move around
all the time.

But if you do this it will be slightly eccentric, or
it might be considered so, and this is a good factor
in a decoration. So the hanging faces may become
basic to a decoration and may be developed with various
other eccentric treatments.

If you make a face deliberately for a hanging
decoration you must be prepared to simplify the
features. Cutting them on the fold from different
coloured papers will usually be effective. Small
cuts at regular intervals into the outer edge of the
face shape, which will allow you to fold the sections
between them alternately forwards and back, will add
to the effect (Fig. 118).

When you make a change like this at the edges of a
shape you will cause interesting shadow and tone
effects on it, and will also introduce more form into
the shape. A face can of course be made on both sides
of the shape.

Like any decoration these can be hung separately
or can be combined into groups as in the illustration.
You will appreciate that if these were strung one
above the other and were hanging freely, they would not
necessarily rotate together, so that you might get
the interesting effect of seeing faces from any position
in the room.

Faces hung together like this would be simple
'mobiles', that is a type of art which is made deliberately so that it is not static.

Mobiles made up from faces can also be used as
decorations, and might be amusing in the way they

188 seem to change expression as they move in space.

A mobile face like one of the decorative ladies illustrated (Fig. 119) could be made up from a number of separate pieces. These could be attached with cotton so that when the face was hung they would all move independently. They should not touch at any point during any part of the movement, as this will inhibit a free and continuous effect in the mobile.

When the separate pieces are joined together—cotton should be strong enough—a final thread can be fixed at the top of the assembly, so that the whole mobile is suspended at this point from one thread. The best method of assembly is to start at the lowest piece and to work upwards to the last thread.

There are many subjects which can form the basis for Mobile faces. Clowns with large noses and lips are an obvious choice (Fig. 120), or ladies with ear-rings and decorative hats, like the example shown in Fig. 121.

If you look at this example of the face mobile you will see that the circular mouth shape is hung from the lower edge of the nose. The nose is fixed with another thread to the top shape. The ear-rings and ears are strung in similar ways, and the eyes are added separately. The shapes do not touch at any point.

The final thread should be fixed at the top of the mobile at the point of balance. If this is not done with some care the whole assembly will flop into a one-sided and shapeless muddle.

To find the point of balance a trial and error method can be used. With a pin, or with the point of a compass, trial holes can be made at the top of the shape to see if it hangs squarely from this point before threading. If the hole is not in the right place the mobile will not be satisfactory, and further exploratory holes must be tried.

For a very simple hanging decoration, paper features can be stuck to inflated balloons with transparent adhesive tape (Fig. 121). These can be made in many different shapes and colours, and at this stage in your work it should be possible to cut and develop the trimmings freehand from oddments of paper left from previous exercises. A nose shape needs to be no more than an inverted triangle, and eyes can be

Fig. 118 Edge cutting and folding of simple face shapes will give them interesting form as hanging decorations.

Fig. 119 Faces can be made up as Mobiles with simple decorative treatments.

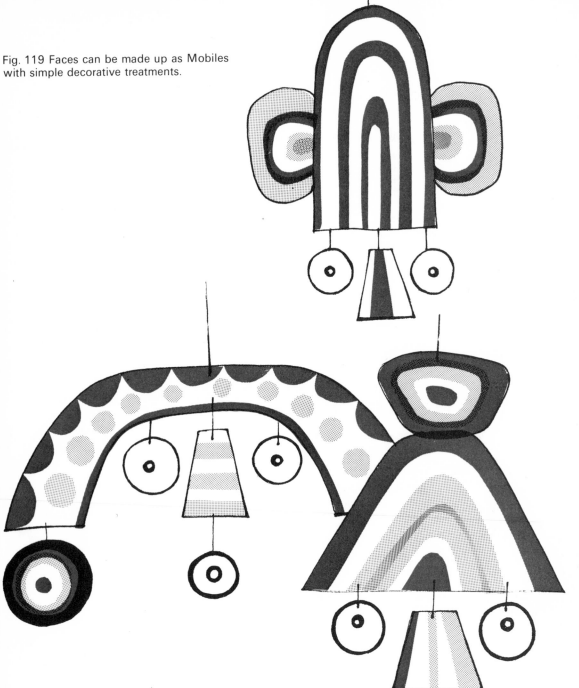

simple white circles with dark pupils.

But by this stage you will not need to be told what to do.

If you have worked through some of the exercises you will know about the material you are using. You will understand some of the ways in which it can

190

Fig. 120 The mobiles made of faces with moving parts can be developed on a variety of subjects.

Fig. 121 Balloons can be used as basic shapes for faces which are to be hung as decorations.

192 be used best, and you will also appreciate some of its limitations.

You will know how to start a project in paper or cardboard, and whether it is possible to find a basic shape to work on.

The book you have just read is really about material and the way it can be made to do things. It takes people as its subject because we all know about them in some detail, and because in the main they are fun. They might be cross and bad tempered sometimes, but they are always in some way interesting. And paper is always available, coloured or patterned—either bought or collected as salvage.

If you put the two together you might find that there are many interesting creative opportunities to be had with—PAPER PEOPLE.

Other books by Michael Grater

—in which the engaging art of paper sculpture is explored
in a way that combines sheer fun with sound and purposeful
educational theory. As well as giving pleasure to children,
they are planned to be of use to art teachers and student
teachers who are looking for new and imaginative approaches
to their work. The books, suitable for any child who is
old enough to be trusted with sharp tools, are of the same
format as PAPER PEOPLE and are also illustrated with the
author's diagrams and with photographs of his work. Here
are some details:

MAKE IT IN PAPER

His first, and a delightful introduction to paper-cutting.
The principles are carefully explained, and the patterns are
graded from the very simple to the more complex; ways of
decorating the paper shapes are suggested.
96 pp. SBN 8008-5050-5 $4.95

ONE PIECE OF PAPER

Offers instructions and diagrams for a varied collection of
creatures which can be cut out of one imperial-sized sheet
(or less). Try the squiggly furry caterpillar, the very
rabbity rabbit, the blissful butterflies (to mention only
a few).
120 pp. SBN 8008-5825-5 $7.50

PAPER FACES

A book of masks. Starting with simple shapes, it builds up
to more complicated masks of birds, animals and people,
which can be decorated to give grotesque and amusing
results.
140 pp. SBN 8008-6250-3 $5.50

We have a wide range of art and craft books,
written by experts and attractively illustrated.
We will be glad to send our list free on application.

TAPLINGER PUBLISHING COMPANY
New York